This book belongs to...

....

CHRIS RIDDELL

ACKNOWLEDGEMENTS

Kids' Night In could not have been accomplished without the time, energy and spirit of so many people. In particular, we cannot thank each and every one of the contributors enough for giving us both their precious time and talent, and producing the masterpieces in this collection. For without them *Kids' Night In* could never have happened.

We would also like to extend heartfelt thanks to those who have helped this book become reality: everyone at Collins Children's Books, especially Alison Stanley, Gillie Russell, Jo Williamson, Caroline Paul, Claire Elliot, Suzanne Harris and Lee Motley; our wonderful agent Jonathan ('J-Lo') Lloyd, Fiona Inglis, Pippa Masson, Tara Wynne and all those at Curtis Brown UK and Australia; the Puffin (Australian) edition editors – Jessica Adams (an inspiration), Nick Earls and Juliet Partridge – and publishers Michelle Madden, Laura Harris and Julie Gibbs; and all our 'fairy godmothers and fathers', who include Maggie Alderson, David Archer, Jaki Archer, Faith Bleasdale, Wendy Bristow, Mary Byrne, the team at Cinemagic Belfast, Clare Conville, Kaz Cooke, Stella Duffy, Imogen Edward-Jones, Josephine Fairley, Eugenie Furniss, Murray Griffin, Nick Hershman, Ineke Hogendijk, Sophie Kinsella, Helen Lederer, Chris Manby, Danny McAull, Philippa Milnes-Smith, Freya North, Tyne O'Connell, Nessa O'Neill, Jane Owen, Francesca Partridge, Anthea Paul, Sophie Ransom, Nick Robertson, Becca Walton, Matthew Wherry, Madeline Wickham, Araminta Whitley, Matt Whyman, Emma Whyman, James Williams and Deborah Wright. Special thanks also to Darren O'Shaughnessy, Matt Foster and Mary & Christine Walsh.

Helen Basini and Sara Walsh
(*Kid's Night In* Project Team, War Child UK)

kids' night in

Brilliant new stories
by favourite authors
published for **WAR** child

Charity No. 1071659

An imprint of HarperCollins*Publishers*

JF
1220416

Tony Hart

First published in Great Britain by Collins in 2003
Collins is an imprint of HarperCollins*Publishers* Ltd,
77 - 85 Fulham Palace Road, Hammersmith, London W6 8JB

The HarperCollins website address is www.**fire**and**water**.co.uk
www.warchild.org.uk

1 3 5 7 9 8 6 4 2

CAT DEELEY
INTRODUCTION

Thank you for buying *Kids' Night In*! You will find some of your favourite authors and illustrators inside, so we hope you like it as much as we do. All these people have given their fantastic stories and drawings for nothing, and even the bookplate at the front (we hope you fill it in) has been donated. By buying *Kids' Night In*, you have already given one pound to War Child, a charity which helps children in countries devastated by war. So thanks to YOU as well. Now, all you have to do is put on your pyjamas, make yourself a hot chocolate, put a 'Do Not Disturb' sign on the door, and settle down with this book for the best kids' night in ever.

CONTENTS

The Real Rebecca	Jacqueline Wilson	9
Bits of an Autobiography	Morris Gleitzman	25
Hagurosan	Darren Shan	34
Mary's Hair	Eoin Colfer	55
Angels' Night Off	Annie Dalton	66
Charlie Rabbit	Garth Nix	79
Sergeant Mugworth and Algy Buttons	Brian Jacques	96
Miss Shush	Brian Patten	124
The Star	Marianne Curley	126
The Cabinet of Curiosities	Philip Ardagh	138
No Place for Frogs	Dick King-Smith	149
Bubble Trouble	Roger McGough	156
For Carlos	Michael Morpurgo	158
The Amazing Furniture Zoo Park	Deborah Wright	168
Racing Guinea Pigs	Georgia Byng	180
Sky Ship	Geraldine McCaughrean	184
This is NOT a Fairy Tale	Jeremy Strong	190
Under the Skin	Celia Rees	202
The Cherry Pie	Ros Asquith	212
The Last Halloween	Rachel Cohn	214
A Letter to the King	Gillian Cross	226
The Misfit	Eva Ibbotson	229
Henry's Guide to the Stars	Jessica Adams	239

Drip, Drip, Drip	Malorie Blackman	**245**
The Shadow Thief	Margaret Mahy	**256**
A Sea Find	Beverley Naidoo	**266**
The Truth About Possums	James Moloney	**270**
Frequent Flyer	Mary Hoffman	**282**
The Mighty One's Daughter	Vivian French	**294**

JACQUELINE WILSON

the real rebecca

ILLUSTRATION BY NICK SHARRATT

101 Newton Street
Kingtown

Dear Jenna Williams,

   I know you probably get hundreds of letters every week. My little sister Molly has written to you in the past. It was the letter with all the glitter (left over from when she made her own Christmas cards) and it said in bright pink gel pen:

Dear Jena
I am your number one fan and you are my favorit writter
lots of love and kisses
from Molly.

It's probably not the most eloquent letter you've ever received but she's only seven and it took her ages. I'm Molly's big brother. I don't want to sound rude, but I'm afraid I'm not your number one fan. I haven't actually read many of your books. Especially not the lovey-dovey girly ones. We *did* read one in Year Five at primary school, the one about the really bad kid who runs away – and did you write that book about the boy who gets ill? If so, I've read that one too. But I'm not really into that sort of real-life stuff, especially not now I'm thirteen.

I like Fantasy. I don't just read it, I write it too. I've made up this entire world, Jakarabia, and I live there, and there are various tribes who live in different parts, the Junglies and the Seaswimmers and the Mountain-Hoppers, and I'm the leader of all of them, and then there are all these different weird animals and some alien creatures too – well, I won't go on about it, you don't want to listen to all *my* stupid story, though actually I tell it to Molly sometimes when she can't sleep at night and she seems to love it. But I think she actually likes your books a bit more. She's got this whole shelf-full and she reads them over and over and colours in all the pictures with her gel pens and sticks gold and silver stars all over the covers.

So when Mum saw you were coming to Kingtown last Saturday to do a book-signing she thought Molly might like to come and meet you.

'Meet *Jenna Williams*?' said Molly, like you were the Queen and David Beckham and Britney Spears all rolled into one person.

'Oh yes please yes please yes please!' I don't get why she got so excited. I mean, no offence, but you don't have a crown and a palace and you don't play football and you can't sing; you're just an ordinary old lady who writes kids' books.

But Molly *likes* your books, and she got so worked up on Friday night she couldn't get to sleep for ages and I had to tell her Jakarabia stories until I was hoarse. In fact I invented an entirely new tribe of Cavedwellers who tell stories all night long and they start off in great booming voices, and finish at dawn in hoarse whispers.

I was still a bit croaky at breakfast on Saturday morning, so I gulped down a little milk to soothe my throat. And a bowl or two of cornflakes to go with it. Mum got a bit narked with me because there wasn't quite enough milk or cornflakes left and she and Molly had to make do with toast and juice.

'You're a hopeless greedy gannet, Jake,' she said crossly. 'I'll have to go shopping now and yet it's not payday till next week.'

We haven't got that much cash. My dad doesn't always send the maintenance money for us when he should. Mum did have a boyfriend for a bit but it didn't work out. Basically, Molly and I couldn't stick him. So now we're back to Mum and Molly and me and we're fine. We're definitely *not* like one of those dysfunctional families in your books. No offence again, but why do you always write about people with problems???

Anyway, we had a slight problem on Saturday morning. I wanted to spend my Saturday slobbing on the sofa, watching telly and maybe writing further chronicles of Jakarabia. But Mum wanted to go shopping and Molly wanted to meet Jenna Williams – you!

'I think there might be a bit of a queue at the bookshop,' said Mum. 'You come with us, Jake. Then you can stand in the queue with Molly while I go and do the shopping. It'll be much quicker that way. And I don't like leaving you in the house by yourself.'

'Mum! I'm not an infant. I'm a *teenager*,' I said, sighing heavily.

'Only just.' Mum came over to me and stood with her hands on her hips, looking down on me. Which is not hard to do. My mum's quite tall. And just at the moment, before my hormones kick in or whatever, I happen to be a tad on the short side. I'm sure any day now I'll shoot up rapidly to at least six foot. It's not for lack of nourishment, as Mum would rapidly agree.

'When you get bigger than me maybe I'll do what *you* say. Up till then, I'm the boss, OK?' said Mum. 'And I say you're coming into town with us, pal.'

'All right. If I must. But I don't want to stand in a queue with a whole lot of *girls*. I'll look such a twit. You stand in the queue, Mum, and *I'll* do the shopping.'

'Oh no. I don't trust you with my housekeeping purse! You'd forget the basics and just buy crisps and coke and chocolate.'

'They're *my* basics.'

'Quite,' said Mum. 'No. I'll shop. You queue.'

'I hate queueing. It makes my legs ache,' I moaned.

'Well, we'll get there early, OK. It shouldn't be *too* long a queue,' said Mum.

Ha ha ha. (The 'ha's' represent mirthless sarcastic laughter.)

We thought we were early. But the world and his wife and their small daughters must have been up at the crack of dawn because as soon as we got into Flowerfields shopping centre we saw this huge great queue snaking out of the first-floor bookshop, right down the stairs and way past the ornamental singing teddies.

'Oh my goodness,' said Mum.

'Oh total *badness*,' I said. 'This is crazy. We're going to be stuck here for hours and hours.'

'Maybe we won't bother,' said Mum. 'Molly, sweetheart, you won't mind terribly if we don't wait all that time, do you? I mean, it isn't really worth it, is it? You don't really need to get Jenna Williams to sign your books?'

We looked at Molly. She'd dressed up specially in her best pink T-shirt with the silver star and she'd smeared silver glitter gel all over her funny little face. She had all her dog-eared Jenna Williams collection crammed into a carrier bag. She was carrying it carefully as if it was the crown jewels. Her eyes blinked as Mum spoke. Her lip started quivering. A tear dripped down her glittery cheek. She didn't say anything. She didn't need to. Molly *would* mind terribly if we didn't wait. She *did* think it was worth it. She needed Jenna Williams to sign *all* her books.

I sighed. Mum sighed.

'OK,' said Mum. 'You join the back of the queue, Jake. I'll go and tackle the shopping. I'll try not to be too long.'

'Take your time,' I said. 'It looks as if Molly and I are going to be stuck here all morning. And afternoon. And most of the evening too.'

I took hold of Molly by her bony little elbow and steered her to the end of the queue, behind a mum in jeans and high heels, a big sister with a tiny top and a little sister with a furry bag bulging with *her* Jenna Williams books.

Mum nodded at the other mum.

'I've got to go and do a bit of shopping. You'll keep an eye on them, won't you?' my mum asked.

'*Mum*!' I hissed. Honestly. I felt so stupid. Mum was acting like I was a little kid. I glared at her. She grinned at me and rushed off. The other mum smiled at me too.

'More Jenna Williams fans?' she said.

'No, absolutely not,' I said quickly. 'I'm just here for my little sister. No, I can't stick Jenna Williams, actually.'

The big sister was looking at me.

And I was looking up at her.

She was GORGEOUS. Very slim, very tall, with a totally wonderfully fantastic figure. Her tight top looked truly astonishing. She was wearing tight jeans too and little slip-on sandals that exposed her perfect, pale feet, each nail polished pink.

Girls with fantastic figures don't always have pretty faces. However, this girl wasn't just pretty, she was beautiful. Utterly beautiful, I tell you, with big blue eyes, tiny nose, rosebud mouth, heart-shaped face and a cloud of curly blonde hair down to her slender shoulders.

I think I am going to invent a princess for Jakarabia. With blue eyes and curly hair. And a fantastic figure. She will of course be mine, because I rule over all Jakarabia, land and sea. So I will take the princess as my royal consort and we will doubtless live happily ever after.

The girl in the queue was a total Princess. But she is not mine and this is not a fairy story so we aren't living happily ever after. *Unless you act as our Fairy Godmother, Jenna Williams!!!*

We got off to a bad start. I'd just said (please don't be hurt) that I didn't rate you or your books, right. This gorgeous girl looked at least fourteen so I was sure she'd be a bit old for them herself. I was convinced she was just in the queue to look out for her little sister, like me. But I was wrong.

'I love Jenna Williams books,' she said.

'Oh. Well. Of course, I'm a boy,' I said. Then I blushed because that was such a daft thing to say. 'I mean, *obviously* I'm a boy, and well, Jenna Williams just writes for girls, doesn't she?'

'I don't think she sets out to write specifically for one sex or the other,' the girl said coolly.

I blushed *again* like a total nerd because she'd said the word sex. I hated myself for acting so stupidly. I'd have given everything to rewind my tape and start over. But this was real life, not the telly. She simply shook her head a little pityingly and turned her back on me. She had a cute little see-through plastic backpack, with three Jenna Williams teenage titles inside.

I wished I'd read the complete works of J.W. and could

discuss them earnestly and intelligently. But I'd obviously blown it.

So I stayed there in the queue with Molly, wishing I was dead. Lots of people came and queued behind us. I soon couldn't see the end of the queue even when I craned my neck. I tried chatting to Molly to pass the time. I offered to tell her a new Jakarabia instalment. I was desperate to show the girl in front that I was a cool, imaginative and caring kind of guy.

But Molly was feeling huffy with me because I'd stupidly said I didn't like boring old Jenna. Whoops! Sorry, no offence intended. You're not the slightest bit boring, I know. And only a little bit old.

'I'm fed up listening to your stories, Jake,' Molly said, sticking her nose in the air. 'I think I'll read one of my Jenna Williams books.'

'Ah. OK. Well, maybe I should give them a go too,' I said. I gave a little cough and raised my voice. 'It would be great if I could have a deck at one of her teenage titles, just to see what I've been missing.'

She *must* have heard me. I was practically bellowing into her ear. Well, I didn't quite reach up to her ear, but I'm speaking figuratively, right. Anyway, she didn't take a blind bit of notice. She just started nattering to her mum, ignoring me. And then her little sister started chatting to Molly, comparing notes on their favourite Jenna Williams books. I just stood there. Not talking to anyone. For hours.

Every quarter of an hour the ornamental clock chimed maddeningly and the teddy bear models started waving their paws and revolving their eyes. Then they started 'singing' in mad growly voices. I've never been very keen on that old song *Teddy Bears' Picnic*. But try having it growled again and again and again. You feel like going down to those woods and biffing them all in their big furry tummies.

I was not a happy guy.

Mum came back with her shopping. She'd got bars of chocolate and coke for Molly and me. She gave some to the Princess and her little sister too. Little sister was called Hannah but for endless ages I didn't have a clue what *big* sister was called. I couldn't get up the nerve to ask her outright.

I know this might strike you as a bit odd because down on paper I am dead articulate. In fact I tend to go on a bit *too* much. This is the ninth page of my letter and I still haven't got to the point. Well, we're nearly there.

When I was nearly in front of you I found out the Princess's name. *You* asked her, as you signed her teenage books. She smiled at you and said she was called Rebecca. Beautiful name. You signed her books and then you signed little Hannah's books and *then* it was Molly's turn. Only you might remember, our Molly suddenly went all white and whimpery and wouldn't budge. I couldn't believe it! Molly's never the slightest bit shy. And we'd waited in your wretched queue for hours and hours and now it looked like she wasn't even going to say hello to you.

So I seized Molly by the wrist and pulled her up to your signing table and Molly hung her head and wouldn't look at you. But it was OK in the end because you started chatting to her, saying you loved her silver glitter and the silver star on her T-shirt and you let her try on one of your silver rings. Do you remember? Molly won't ever forget. You signed her books and she skipped all the way home, even though her legs must have been aching after all that queuing.

I trudged home. My legs were certainly aching. And my heart.

I had hoped to catch up with Rebecca and ask her out. But by the time Molly had cheered up and got all her books signed Rebecca and Hannah and their mum had disappeared out of the shop.

I'd lost my chance. I'd had hours and hours when I could have asked her but I just couldn't get up the courage. I'm just a hopeless wimp.

So how about helping me out, Jenna Williams??? I know you've got your own website. Please can you tell my story and ask any stunningly beautiful tall teenage girl called Rebecca (with a little sister called Hannah) who was in that ludicrously long queue at Kingtown to get in touch with me, as I care about her passionately and am desperate to see her again. Please please please!

In feverish anticipation

Jake Wilson

haphazardhouse
children's books

Dear Jake,

Thank you so much for your letter. I enjoyed reading it enormously. I shall keep it carefully and then when you're a best-selling fantasy author I shall boast that I have a very special letter written by you.

If you look on my website you will see that I have indeed told your story – and if Rebecca writes then I will put you in touch with each other, so long as your mums give their permission. Fingers crossed! I love the idea of being a Fairy Godmother.

Give my love to Molly.

All good wishes

Jenna Williams

13 Feltham Drive
Kingtown

Dear Jenna Williams,

This is so weird! I am a big fan of your books and so I very happily queued for ages and ages when you came to Kingtown the other week. Of course you won't remember me, but I was the one with fair curls exploding all over the place and a too-small T-shirt and my mum embarrassed me by telling you I wanted to be a writer too. But you were ever so encouraging and you signed my books and you signed my little sister Hannah's books too.

I'm Rebecca — so this is why I'm writing to you! I read all about this boy Jake on your website.

Don't tell him, but I don't even remember seeing him in the queue! I've been racking my brains and I can't think of <u>any</u> boy standing behind me. But he must have been there because he knows all about me! Admittedly his descriptions of me are exaggerated in the extreme. I am NOT NOT NOT a gorgeous princess and my figure is certainly not fabulous. I'm not tall and slender, I'm small and a bit dumpy. But I don't mind a bit that Jake seems to think I look OK! Please put me in touch with him.

Love from
Rebecca

101 Newton Street
Kingtown

Dear Jenna Williams,

Oh Woe!

She was the *wrong* Rebecca.

She was OK. I mean, she was actually quite good fun to talk to. Weirdly enough, I didn't feel a bit shy with her. I nattered on like anything. I even told her about Jakarabia and she seemed quite interested. She writes too. She actually came up with some relatively interesting ideas that might well get incorporated in future Jakarabia tales.

But it was all a bit pointless because she *isn't* the Princess of my dreams. She's just this ordinary bit-plumpish fair thirteen-year-old.

So where is the *real* Rebecca???? I will languish after my Princess for ever and a day. It is my fate.

Yours, in despair

Jake Wilson

xxxxxx These aren't from me, they're from Molly.

haphazardhouse
children's books

Dear Jake,

Oh woe too!

I had a feeling she might well be the wrong Rebecca. It's a very common name (though beautiful). Ditto Hannah. And she certainly didn't sound a vision of beauty. But do you know why I put you in touch with her? Because I couldn't help wondering if she might be the RIGHT Rebecca for you. I should meet up with her again!

I don't think it's a good idea to languish after the real Rebecca. I am not an Agony Aunt but I can't resist reminding you that Princesses can sometimes turn out to be frogs – even totally gorgeous ones with fabulous figures. And you thought she was at least fourteen, so she's technically an Older Woman. Maybe this bothers her. She didn't sound especially warm and friendly to you. There's another slightly delicate point. You mentioned she was tall. Perhaps it might be a little uncomfortable if she looked down on you, both figuratively and literally. Remember how irritating this is when your mum does it!

Perhaps Fate decreed that you and the other funny friendly Rebecca were right for each other but it would have been too predictably boring to have a Boy meets

Girl/Boy loses Girl/Boy finds Girl story. If I were writing your story I'd much prefer the twist of Boy meets Girl/Boy loses Girl/Boy doesn't find Girl/Boy finds another Girl.

What do you think?

All good wishes

Jenna Williams

XXXXXXXXXXXXXXXXXXXXXXXXXXXXXXXX

for Molly

101 Newton Street
Kingtown

13 Feltham Drive
Kingtown

Dear Old Agony Aunty Jenna,

If your books stop selling some day maybe you could become a real Agony Aunt because you give really good advice!

We are best friends now and we meet up nearly every day. We are writing a brand new story together. It's a fantasy story. We don't write real-life stuff. But you do. We wondered if you might like to write *our* story?

Yours very happily indeed

Jake and Rebecca

kids' night in

haphazardhouse
children's books

Dear Jake and Rebecca,

Maybe I *will* write your story. And we'll get Molly to
illustrate it with silver glitter hearts!

With very very best wishes

Jenna Williams

MORRIS GLEITZMAN

bits of an autobiography I may not write

Two weeks of thinking, and still no idea for my next book. I'd tried everything. Meditation. Self-hypnosis. Vacuuming my scalp to stimulate my brain.

Then a letter arrived from a kid in Western Australia. 'Your books are pretty good,' she wrote, 'except for the total lack of motorbikes.'

I fell to my knees, partly in gratitude and partly because the vacuum cleaner was still on my head. At last, a story idea. A kid travelling across the Great Sandy Desert on a motorbike. Not bad.

I'd just finished chapter one when the next letter came.

'Reasonably OK books,' wrote a kid in Adelaide, 'but why so few exotic fish?'

Good point. I rewrote chapter one. It ended up longer, mostly because the bike couldn't travel so fast with the aquarium on the back.

'Your stories would be more interesting,' said a letter from Bristol, 'if they included more elderly people.'

I had to agree. I rewrote chapter one and it certainly was more interesting. Particularly when one of the kid's grandparents, parched from running to keep up with the bike, drank the aquarium and swallowed a coral trout.

It looked like she was a goner until the letter from Philadelphia arrived. 'More sports,' it said. Which is how, in the next draft, the kid came to have a table-tennis bat handy to whack Gran on the back.

'Shouldn't you be thinking up your own ideas, Dad?' asked the kids.

'Why?' I replied.

'Oh, no reason,' they shrugged, handing me six letters.

'Water-skiing,' said one. 'Clydesdale horses,' said another. 'Self-reticulating irrigation systems,' said the other four.

This morning when the postman came I hid under my desk. He found me. I was sobbing.

'Must be tough, being a writer,' he said, bending down and handing me a bundle of letters. 'I wouldn't know where to get the ideas from.'

*   *   *

It was a proud moment. I'd just built my first piece of furniture and I could feel my chest swelling almost as much as the finger I'd hit with the hammer.

'Well,' I said to the kids, 'what do you think?'

I held my breath as they ran their hands over the four sturdy legs, the finely stitched upholstery and the skilfully hung mirrored door.

'Funny looking bookshelves, Dad,' they said. My chest deflated. They were right. Who was I trying to kid? I was a writer, not a handyman.

'Do-it-yourself furniture,' I said bitterly. 'If there's anyone who can build this stuff themselves I'd like to know their secret.'

The kids looked at the empty boxes strewn around the room. 'Perhaps,' they said gently, 'it involves assembling the bookcase, the settee, the coffee table and the bathroom cabinet as four separate items.'

'It was the instructions,' I said. 'They were impossible to understand. Look at that diagram. I broke three screwdrivers trying to follow that.'

The kids sighed. 'It's the furniture-shop logo,' they said.

I realised my problem was that I didn't speak the language of do-it-yourself. I started at language school the following week. The other students were doing French, Spanish and Japanese. I enrolled in Furniture Assembly.

The instructor tried hard, but by the ninth week I still couldn't translate 'slot base support bracket A into side panel rib B'. I couldn't even say it.

'I'm sorry,' said the instructor, 'I can't do any more for you.'

I looked at him pleadingly. 'Not even put my bookshelves together?'

He shook his head.

At home I stared gloomily at the bookshelf assembly instructions. Why could I construct a story but not a piece of furniture? Then I noticed the instructions were looking different. They were in the kids' handwriting. 'One fine day,' I read excitedly, 'a base support bracket named A met a side panel rib called B...'

Drop in and see my new bookshelves some time. They look great.

*   *   *

The kids stared at the peanut butter, beetroot, sardine and pineapple sandwich.

'Dad,' they pleaded, 'couldn't you make it plain old cheese and tomato?'

I put the sandwich into the lunch box and explained that I'd decided to make something special for the first day.

'But this isn't our first day,' said the kids. 'We've been going to school for years.'

I added a kiwi fruit, two gherkins and some kangaroo salami to the lunch box. 'It's my new book's first day,' I said, voice trembling. 'At the publisher's.'

The kids stared at the manuscript. They stared at the woolly scarf tied round it and the knitted hat pulled down snugly over the title page. Then they stared at me. 'You're making your new book a packed lunch?' they croaked.

'Please,' I said. 'It isn't easy, saying goodbye to a manuscript. Sending it off to that big scary building. It's almost as upsetting as your first day at school and you remember how upsetting that was.'

The kids said they did, particularly the sandwiches.

My eyes misted over. 'It's only a ninety-six-page kids' book,' I sobbed as I filled its plastic drink bottle. 'What if it gets bullied by a 600-page truck repair manual?'

The kids took me to one side. 'Dad,' they said quietly, 'remember how you were a bit over-protective when we started school? Getting your helicopter licence and joining the traffic police so you could hover over the playground at lunchtime?'

I pulled myself together. 'It's OK,' I said. 'I'm not going to embarrass my new book like that.'

And I meant it. Which is why I got the job as the window cleaner. Far less noticeable and I was still able to keep an eye on my baby from the extension ladder.

That's how I was the first to know about the tragedy. The publishers decided to delay publication of my new manuscript. First they made me write them a sandwich recipe book.

* * *

The judge looked sternly down at me. 'You have been charged,' he said, 'with one of the most serious crimes ever to be tried in this courtroom. How do you plead?'

The public gallery was packed and the jury was staring at me accusingly. My mouth felt like a sandpit in the Simpson Desert.

'Not guilty,' I croaked. 'I'm innocent. I didn't do it. Honest.'

The prosecutor was on her feet. 'I put it to you,' she said, 'that last April fourteenth at bedtime you read your children *The Twits* by Roald Dahl and that you wilfully and intentionally left out the bit about the wormy spaghetti because you didn't want to miss the start of the wrestling on telly.'

'Not true,' I cried. 'It wasn't wrestling, it was showjumping.'

The public gallery gasped. The jury narrowed their eyes. I put my head in my hands.

'All right,' I sobbed, 'I admit it. I couldn't bear to read it all again. I'd read it 127 times in the past year alone.'

My kids took the witness stand. 'That wasn't the worst example,' they said. 'In May he read us *War and Peace* and all we got was "Once upon a time there was a war, and then there was peace, the end."'

'I couldn't stand it again,' I sobbed, 'not for the eleventh time.'

'And that,' said the prosecutor, 'was the same week he read you *Ode to a Nightingale*?'

The kids looked at me sadly. 'He said it was Keats,' they murmured, 'but we just didn't think that "Tweet, tweet, OK kids time to settle down now, *The Bill*'s started" sounded much like a classic poem.'

It was a long trial. I was found guilty. I anxiously studied the judge's wig, hoping to see the telltale sticky fingermarks that would reveal he understood what it was to be a parent. There weren't any. So when he read out my jail sentence he didn't skip a single bit. But then he was only eleven.

* * *

'Dad,' said the kids, 'why are you kneeling on the floor with your head in the fridge? Have you got a headache?'

I explained I hadn't, I was just telling the tops of the plastic salad containers about my schooldays.

The kids both stared at me.

'It's one of my New Year resolutions,' I explained, showing them the list I'd made. 'See? Number four.'

'*Spend more time talking to the kids*,' read the ten-year-old.

I took the list back. 'Does it say kids?' I said, squinting at it. 'I could have sworn it said lids.'

The kids sighed. So did the lids.

'Pity you haven't kept the first New Year resolution on your list,' said the kids.

'I have,' I said, squeaking to my feet and showing them my bright yellow rubber footwear. 'See? *Get new galoshes*.'

The kids sighed again. 'Dad,' they groaned, pointing to the list. 'It says *get new glasses*.'

'Oh dear,' I said, squinting again at the blurry writing. A chill crept up my spine and not just because I'd left the fridge door open. 'Um,' I said, 'I'm feeling a bit bad now about New Year resolutions two and three.'

The kids studied the list. '*Two*,' they read, '*polish the car*. What's wrong with that?'

I took them outside and pointed up to the roof. 'There's no car up there,' said the kids. Then they saw the shiny cat.

The cat slid off the roof, leaving a trail of Supa-Shine wax on the tiles. The kids caught it, glared at me and we went inside.

'Number three can't be worse than that,' they said. I could feel a headache coming on, so I put my head in the fridge.

The kids read out number three. '*Get more sleep*. What's so bad about that?'

I closed my eyes, laid my head down next to the lettuce and waited for them to hear the baa-ing coming from the living room.

* * *

It had been a hard day and now, as I slumped wearily down at the dinner table, the kids were staring at me.

'What's the matter,' I said, 'haven't you ever seen a bloke with oil on his hands and grease in his armpits and soot on his face and electrical burns on his scalp?'

'Not one that says he's a children's author,' they replied accusingly. 'You've been fibbing to us, haven't you Dad? You don't write kids' books at all, you lubricate heavy mining equipment.'

I sighed and took them into my study. 'The days are gone,' I said, 'when all you needed to write a book was a pencil and six rolls of toilet paper. It's a high-tech business these days, being an author. And some days you trip over the computer cable and slosh coffee into the printer and the explosion sends you reeling back into the photocopier, which short-circuits the fax machine and melts the modem.'

The kids looked at the smoking wreckage. 'What you need,'

they said, 'is to get back in touch with the simple things in life. Why don't you take up gardening?'

My motto is try anything once unless it gives you dandruff, so the next morning I put on an old jumper and went out the back to grow things.

The kids appeared a couple of hours later. 'Dad,' they yelled, 'what are you doing?'

I paused to wipe the sump oil out of my ears. 'Planting carrots,' I said, 'but first I have to clear these weeds.'

I realise now it was taking my hand off the chainsaw that allowed it to rear up and knock the flame-thrower against the handbrake of the bulldozer.

I'm in hospital now and it's great. I've been on the X-ray machine and the ultrasound machine and the electrocardiogram machine, and tomorrow they're putting me on the brain-scan machine. I'm looking forward to that. Just as long as the doctor doesn't spill his coffee.

DARREN SHAN

hagurosan

NO PATH IS ORDINARY / ALL ARE
MAGICAL / WINDING THEIR WAYS
TO WONDERS

'I don't want to go to the shrine,' Hagurosan said. 'I want to play.'

'There will be time to play later,' his mother replied, handing him a small, freshly baked cake. 'Take this and offer it to the spirits.'

'But—' Hagurosan began.

'Please,' his mother sighed. 'I am too tired to argue.'

And because Hagurosan was a good child, he pulled a face, stuck the cake in his pocket, and set off on the hour-long walk to the shrine.

The sun sizzled in the sky. Children were playing in the dust, splashing each other with water from the well. Some of Hagurosan's friends saw him. 'Come play with us!' they called. But Hagurosan shook his head and walked on.

Hagurosan scaled the small hill overlooking his village. He paused to admire the round huts and thatched roofs, then trotted down the gentle slope to the base of the Holy Mountain, where the real climb began.

The gods dwelt on top of the cloud-capped mountain. The clouds were their floors. When the sky was blue, it meant they were abroad. Only the priests climbed to the top of the Holy Mountain. It was guarded by snake-hounds, which would kill any human foolish enough to disobey the sacred laws.

But there was a shrine a fifth of the way up, where the spirits lived. Hagurosan wasn't entirely sure about the ways in which spirits were different from gods, but he knew they weren't as powerful. They were also more involved with humans. Gods only intervened on important occasions, during war, or if the land was threatened by disease. The spirits, on the other hand, could protect a farmer's crops, or ensure a woman's birthing time went smoothly.

The climb was hard. Although the path was lined with trees, the sun found a way through, and Hagurosan was soon sweating. He stopped by a stream to wash his face and drink. The stream was a fierce torrent in winter, but today it was a bare trickle.

As Hagurosan rested, he saw a bird overturn a pebble and greedily peck at the insects underneath. Hagurosan's stomach rumbled. Many splendid fruits grew on the Holy Mountain, but all were forbidden to the villagers. Only the priests could harvest the crops here.

Hagurosan's right hand stole to his pocket. 'I can't eat the cake,' he muttered. 'Not all of it. But the spirits won't mind if I take a small bite.' He pulled out the cake and nibbled at a corner. Then he nibbled at the other corners, to make it look as though the cake was designed with four in-slanting corners. Pleased with this, he went to replace the cake in his pocket. But, because he did not want to damage it, he decided to leave it safe in his hand. He continued up the Holy Mountain.

Unfortunately for Hagurosan, a cake in a boy's hand has the knack of finding its way to his lips. As he climbed, he nibbled; a bit here, a bit there. He meant to leave a large chunk, but by the time he arrived at the shrine, only crumbs remained, stuck to his fingers like glittering brown stars. And even these he licked clean before entering the shrine, so that he could place his hands together cleanly and pray.

Short stone statues dotted the shrine's circular bounds. Larger statues adorned the interior. The largest was at the centre, twice Hagurosan's height. All of the statues had faces which were human and yet not. Most had been wrapped in layers of clothing – a cape, a hat, a shawl. Toys lay at the feet of some statues, or tools, or coins. (There were not many coins. Hagurosan came from a poor village. They bartered with other villages for most of their goods.) Food – mostly rotting cakes – surrounded every statue. All of the goods had been left as offerings to the spirits.

Hagurosan's family usually left their offerings at the feet of a statue near the rear of the shrine. It had been erected by Hagurosan's great-grandfather, and it was supposed to look like him. But today Hagurosan dared not face that statue. He had eaten the offering and it was only now he was standing within the shrine that he realised the size of his sin. He had taken food meant for the spirits. People who did that were struck down dead or inflicted with a terrible disease. Sometimes their families were cursed, too.

Hagurosan thought about running away and lying to his mother, but the spirits could not be tricked. His only hope was to throw himself at their mercy and pray that they took pity on him.

Hagurosan walked to the statue at the centre of the shrine, head bowed and hands joined, murmuring prayers. When he reached the statue, he fell to his knees and prayed for several minutes, before looking up at the weather-beaten face.

'I didn't mean to eat the cake,' Hagurosan said, a tear trickling from his left eye. 'I only wanted a bit of it. But I couldn't stop once I started.' He rooted through his pockets, looking for something else to offer the spirits. But his pockets were empty. He thought about taking off his shorts and leaving them, but that would mean walking naked back to the village.

'Please don't curse me,' Hagurosan whimpered. 'If you forgive me, I'll come back with all my toys. I'll give you all my dinners for a week. Anything!'

A light breeze whistled through the trees, but that was the only response. Hagurosan stood uncertainly. 'If you curse me,' he said to the statue, 'will you please not curse my family? They didn't eat the cake. That was just me.'

Hagurosan made for the exit. He was almost there when something twinkled and caught his eye. Stopping, he bent over and discovered a small silver coin nestled in a bed of moss.

Hagurosan's heart beat fast with excitement. A real silver coin! He'd never held one before. A copper coin, yes, a couple of times. But never silver. His head spun giddily as he thought of all the things he could buy. Toys, sweet cakes, clothes. A present for his mother. She loved it when his father returned from market with presents. It didn't happen very often, but when it did she smiled her widest smile and was in a good mood for days after.

Gripping the coin tight, Hagurosan started forward at a run...

Then stopped. He opened his hand slowly and gazed down at the coin, then looked back at the tall statue in the centre of the shrine. Although he knew it was impossible, Hagurosan had the feeling that the statue's eyes had moved. They seemed to be focused on him now, judging him.

'OK,' Hagurosan sighed after a handful of seconds. He trudged unhappily back to the statue, knelt, and set the coin down before it. There weren't many offerings here, but all were impressive – a beautiful mirror, ornate necklaces, a leather wallet, and several sparkling jewels. Only the best gifts were left at this statue, on occasions when people had something extra special to wish for.

'There,' Hagurosan said. 'It's worth much more than the cake. You could buy a hundred cakes with it. But it's yours now. I don't deserve it.'

He glanced up at the statue, hoping it would come to life, smile upon him, and tell him that he could keep the coin. But the statue did not move. After one last lingering gaze at the coin,

Hagurosan rose. He was on his feet before it occurred to him that he hadn't made a wish. With so generous a gift, Hagurosan should have been able to make a momentous wish. But, since the gift had been offered to atone for eating the cake, maybe he didn't have the right to wish for anything. At the same time, it would be a shame to waste such a precious wish.

'I know,' he said, suddenly inspired. 'Bless the children of the world, especially those in need of help. Look after them and grant them happiness and a safe place to live. This is my wish.'

Hagurosan bowed low to the statue, turned and walked towards the exit. But this time, as before, he stopped short. There was another coin! It lay in almost the same place, and looked very much like the first coin. Hagurosan felt faint. To find two silver coins in the same day was unheard of!

As Hagurosan picked up the coin, his features creased with doubt. Was this a gift from the spirits? Were they rewarding him for giving the other coin to them? Or was it just good luck? If it was luck, then he should give this one to the spirits as well. He still felt guilty. If he took this coin, the guilt would grow within him and eat him away as surely as he'd eaten the cake.

'This has taught me a lesson I'll never forget!' Hagurosan grunted as he took the coin to the statue and dropped it beside the first coin. He felt disgusted, but he knew he was doing the right thing.

Hagurosan headed for the exit, faster than before, eager to race down the Holy Mountain and tell his friends what had happened. But, for the third time that day, he stopped before setting foot outside the shrine.

There was *another* coin, nestled on its side in the moss!

This time Hagurosan didn't touch the coin. He stared at it suspiciously, afraid. This wasn't normal. It wasn't just that he'd found three silver coins in the same spot on the same day, but that he had not noticed the second and third while picking up the first. Hagurosan now searched around the ground, scattering the moss, sweeping through the dirt, making sure there were no other coins. Satisfied that this was the final one, he took it to the statue, set it down next to the others and again went to leave.

There was another coin.

Hagurosan stood over the coin, shivering. He studied it for what felt like a year, his stomach tight with fear. Then he stepped over it and hurried for the exit.

'**Wait**,' said a voice that was all voices.

Hagurosan froze.

'**We do not want you to leave**,' said the voice that was all voices.

Hagurosan managed to turn his head. He thought he would see the lips of the giant statue moving, but they didn't. None of the statues' lips moved. But words came nevertheless.

'**We want you to collect the coins**,' said the voice that was all voices. '**When the day comes that you see no coin, you may leave with our blessing.**'

'Wh-wh-wh-what if I... luh-luh-leave before that?' Hagurosan croaked.

'**Then we cannot grant your wish**,' said the voice that was all voices, and after that it was silent.

Late that night, Hagurosan's father came looking for him. He found his son huddled on the ground in front of the shrine's largest statue, crying softly. 'Hagurosan,' he said, touching the boy's trembling back. 'What is wrong?'

'The spirits won't let me go!' Hagurosan moaned, clutching his father tightly. 'I ate their cake and now they say I've got to stay here to make my wish come true. But I don't want it to come true, not if it means I can't go home!'

Hagurosan's father let the boy babble, then worked the full story out of him. He was troubled by his son's tale. His first thought was that Hagurosan had made it up. But he could see the three silver coins lying together at the statue's feet.

'Where did you find the coins?' Hagurosan's father asked. When Hagurosan showed him, he searched the ground thoroughly to make sure it was clear. 'Now,' he said, smiling at his son. 'You don't see any coins, do you?'

'No,' Hagurosan sniffed.

'Then come with me.' Hagurosan's father held his hands out.

Hagurosan took a step towards his father. A second. A third. Then he stopped, bent and picked up a dull silver coin. 'See?' he said quietly, turning to place the coin before the statue with the others.

Hagurosan's father studied his son in wonder, then spun round wildly and ran down the Holy Mountain to fetch the local priest.

* * *

The priest was sceptical (and angry at having been disturbed during his supper). But when he saw Hagurosan produce eight silver coins in a row, his scepticism gave way to awe.

'It is a miracle,' the priest said to Hagurosan's father and the scattering of villagers who'd got wind that something strange was happening. 'But I cannot make sense of it. I will need to consult with my superiors.'

'But they are several days' walk away,' Hagurosan's father said. 'What will my son do in the meantime?'

'Stay here,' the priest said. 'And pick coins. As many as he can.'

The priest departed, sweeping down the Holy Mountain, robes flapping around him. Hagurosan's father held a quick conference with the other villagers. Clothes were bundled together and passed to Hagurosan. 'You must sleep here,' his father said.

'What about you?' Hagurosan asked. 'Will you stay, too?'

'I cannot,' his father said. 'It is forbidden for ordinary people to spend the night here. But I will return in the morning and bring your mother.'

Hagurosan's father hugged him hard, then left with the other villagers. Hagurosan felt terribly lonely. He wished with all his heart to race after them. But he didn't dare disobey the will of the spirits, so he pulled the clothes tightly around his body and tried to rock himself to sleep.

Hagurosan's mother marched up the Holy Mountain the next morning, determined to return to the village with her son. But when she saw him pick coins out of what had moments before been thin air, she realised her son was at the centre of something wondrous. Instead of removing Hagurosan from the shrine, she comforted him as best she could, gave him biscuits, and promised to return later with fresh cakes and bread, fish and meat, whatever he desired.

Over the next few days, the people in the village took turns to carry food up the Holy Mountain to Hagurosan. They also brought clothes and toys. Many children came to play with him. They felt awkward around him at first – they had heard their parents talking of a boy marvel – but after a few minutes they saw that he was the same Hagurosan as always, and played with him freely.

When he wasn't playing with his friends, Hagurosan picked coins. He lost count halfway through the second day, but the pile was soon as high as his knees. The villagers reckoned he must have picked five or six hundred silver coins – a fortune.

Each time Hagurosan found a coin, he prayed that it would be the last. But every time he tried to leave, a new coin was waiting to be added to the ever-growing pile at the foot of the statue.

Twelve days later the priest and his superiors returned. The villagers had never seen so many priests before, or such important ones. Most were scared of them and stayed within their huts, fearful lest the priests should mark this as a bad omen and bring a curse upon the entire village.

At the shrine, the braver villagers were told to leave, then the priests entered and positioned themselves in a large circle around Hagurosan. Once he'd demonstrated his ability to find magical coins, and once the priests had tried and failed, they questioned him aggressively. Some shouted, some whispered, some threatened, some offered bribes. Hagurosan was terrified and confused by the attention, but all he could do was tell the truth, so he did.

Eventually an elderly priest, who had not yet spoken, cleared his throat. The other priests fell silent. 'This boy has been blessed with punishment,' the priest said calmly. 'The spirits have asked him to collect the coins in order to grant the wish he made. Hagurosan asked them to bless the children of the world, to help and protect those in need. This they are doing, by providing us with the means to help the children ourselves. The coins are for the children,' the priest concluded. 'Hagurosan will collect them, then we will take them and spend them on children who need help.'

'But it is forbidden to remove offerings from the shrine,' another priest said.

'Yes,' the elderly priest agreed. 'But the coins are not our offerings to the spirits. They are the spirits' offerings to us.'

The elderly priest looked at Hagurosan. His eyes were dark and deep, and Hagurosan found himself unable to look away. 'You do not have to do this,' the priest said. 'The spirits did not order you to stay. They said they *wanted* you to collect the coins. If you choose to leave, I do not think they will harm you. But there will be no more coins, and the children you wished to help will suffer.'

Hagurosan almost fled when he heard that. He hadn't really thought about what he was saying when he made the wish, and had no desire to sacrifice his freedom to help others. But now that he considered the priest's words, he realised how instrumental he could be. War and disease were common in his part of the world. There were many orphans, alone and hungry, doomed to die of starvation and lack of care. He had the power to help them. If he turned his back on it, he would feel like the most wretched person on the face of the planet.

'OK,' Hagurosan said, with a heavy heart and tears in his eyes. 'I'll stay.' And as he said it, he imagined a prison door clanging shut behind him, cutting him off from the world for the rest of his life.

NO MATTER THE CREEDS OF MAN / RESPECT THE HOLY / AND THE WORLD IS YOUR REWARD

'*You're* the green-tooth monster!' a young boy shouted, slapping Hagurosan hard. Hagurosan bared his teeth, grunted monstrously, and lumbered after the children, who ran away from him, laughing with delight.

Hagurosan was a young man now. Other men his age were hunting and farming, travelling to market to trade their goods, making plans to marry. Hagurosan, however, remained in the shrine, playing with children, hearing all about the great world beyond from those who visited him, but unable to set foot in it.

He knew every last inch of the shrine. He had walked around it thousands of times. He knew every crack in every statue. He knew the birds, foxes and squirrels that came to feed on the offerings left for the spirits. They had been wary of him to begin with, but now accepted him as just another feature of the shrine.

The village at the foot of the Holy Mountain had changed beyond recognition, according to the reports. The coins Hagurosan collected had been spent well. Shelters had been built to house children who were victims of war or suffering. New bakeries had been established. Public baths. Playgrounds. Even a school!

The village elders relied heavily on Hagurosan for advice. They asked for his counsel before embarking on building schemes. He had been blessed by the spirits, and they did not care to risk offending them by somehow offending Hagurosan.

When Hagurosan wasn't discussing plans with the elders, or collecting coins, he was usually playing or talking with the children. They loved him. Many were suspicious, scared and surly when they came to the village. Hagurosan put them all at their ease. He was able to communicate with them, even if they didn't speak his language – another gift from the gods. He would talk with them when they came, tell them about his past and the village, and gradually chip away at their wounded defences. They learnt first to trust Hagurosan, and later to trust others.

In return for helping them, the children provided Hagurosan with company. It was lonely on the Holy Mountain, but the children helped the days pass quickly. He could not escape the loneliness of the nights, when he slept alone in the small shack which had been built for him within the shrine, but days never dragged.

Sometimes Hagurosan envied his young friends. His heart often ached when he thought of his lost childhood. He would have given anything to be one of those he helped, to be able to explore the village, run where he wished, hunt with the men, trade at market, court girls.

But he never regretted his decision. Almost every day new children arrived, strays and waifs, some travelling for months on end to find refuge, crossing war zones, braving forests filled with wild animals and soul-sucking ghosts. Children without parents and homes, who'd been orphaned or abandoned, some on crutches, some who had crawled; all hurting in one way or another. They were lost, unsure of the world, regarding it warily through haunted, distrustful eyes.

Before, these children would have perished, or grown up into unpleasant, hate-filled adults, twisted by bitterness and lack of love. Now they had a corner of the world to call their own. They were housed, fed, clothed, educated, loved. They played with the children of the village and grew happy and strong. Smiles replaced tears and hope replaced fears.

Whenever Hagurosan felt sad or resentful, he looked into the eyes of the rescued children, saw the relief and happiness, and knew with all his being that he had made the right decision. The knowledge didn't make the regrets go away, but it allowed Hagurosan to live content with them.

One day, priests climbed the Holy Mountain, intent on taking Hagurosan away. They had been sent by a prince from the far north. He wished to install Hagurosan in his palace and use the coins to build temples to his own spirits.

'But what about the children?' Hagurosan cried. 'The spirits provide me with the coins to help them.'

'No,' the head priest said. 'That was a misunderstanding. The spirits wish to be honoured. They would not waste such a fortune on simple children.'

'But they're not wasting it,' Hagurosan said.

'You are a peasant,' the priest laughed. 'What makes you think you know more than us? We have devoted our lives to understanding the ways of the spirits and interpreting their wishes.'

'But—' Hagurosan began.

'Come!' the priest snapped. 'Do not argue. Leave with us now or else—

'**It is not for you to understand the ways of the spirits**,' interrupted a voice that was all voices. Hagurosan had heard this voice before, and smiled. But the priests had never heard it, and they cringed with fear. '**The people we speak to hear us in their hearts and have no need of interpreters. Hagurosan is doing** our work. Let him be, and never again presume to know our thoughts.'

The voice that was all voices stopped. Moments later the priests fled, pale and shaken. They never returned, but word spread of what had happened, and in the years to come more and more people made the pilgrimage to the Holy Mountain, to learn from the man who had heard the spirits with his heart. Hagurosan had only one thing to teach them, since there was only one thing he knew: 'Be kind to the children, and protect them.' But that, as most came to see as they wandered through the village of vibrant, warm-hearted children, was enough. If they could get that right, all else would one day follow.

NEVER DOUBT THE GLORIOUS / It
REVEALS ITSELF / AS TIME RIDS
OUR SOULS OF FLESH

Many years passed. Hagurosan's parents died, along with his friends. He became an elder, one of the oldest ever known. He moved slowly now, and creaked when he bent to pick up the coins. He did not need to sleep much at night, or eat much.

He was enjoying this phase of his life. Every morning he would wake early and collect coins. Shortly after dawn, children from the town started to arrive and he would pass the day talking and playing with them. (The village had grown over the decades, and was now one of the biggest towns in the land.)

Hagurosan never tired of the children. Adults came to see him, too, and he received them politely, but he preferred the company of children. Perhaps it was that he had never really grown out of his own childhood. In some ways he had been robbed of it. He had not matured the same way as other children, learning the ways of adults. Inside he was still a child, seeing the world through fresh, hungry, enquiring eyes.

Nobody knew how many children had been helped by Hagurosan's coins. Thousands, certainly. Tens of thousands, quite possibly. Perhaps more. They had come from all corners of the world, braving the harshest terrains, to find friends and protectors, comfort and rest. They were safe here. The town was a haven. No tribes attacked Hagurosan's people, or made claims on the area. It was a holy place, respected by all, where children could play and grow. No war, no suffering, no hatred, no greed. There was enough for all, and all shared equally.

As the children grew, some married and stayed in the town, while some moved away to lead ordinary lives elsewhere. But others left on a mission. They walked from town to town, village to village, spreading the legend of Hagurosan and sowing the seeds of an idea. 'This does not have to be a one-off,' they told people. 'Children from all over the world have come together and created an earthly paradise. If that can happen in one village, why not in all?'

Hagurosan didn't think the world was ready for the message. He thought people had a long way to go before they were ready to accept the idea that they had the power to create a perfect world. But it was a start. Mankind, like the children of the town, would grow and learn, and perhaps, many years in the future, all villages and towns would be like Hagurosan's. No wars would be fought, and no child or person need ever suffer or go hungry or lonely again.

Hagurosan was talking with some of his many children. They were telling him the latest news from the town. He always enjoyed hearing about the town, even though he often felt a pang of envy and wished he too could walk the streets and enjoy what he had helped create. But the pang was usually a small one, and he had long since learnt to ignore it.

Today, however, as the children were speaking, a sharp pain shot through his chest. He was surprised by it, and upset at himself for being so foolish. To shake off the feeling, he walked towards the exit, meaning to pick up some coins. But when he got to the spot where the coins appeared, there was nothing. He stopped, confused, then took a few paces forward in case he had misjudged the spot. Still no coin.

Hagurosan turned to ask the children if they had played a trick on him and moved the exit. But what he saw caused the words to die on his lips. By the giant statue in the centre of the glade, the children were gathered around the body of a man who was quite obviously dead.

That man was Hagurosan.

As Hagurosan watched, the children wept and stroked the hair and face of the elderly corpse. Two of them hurried down the Holy Mountain to alert their elders. The rest stayed to keep Hagurosan's body company.

'Can I leave now?' Hagurosan asked, his words softer than a light spring breeze.

'**Yes**,' said the voice that was all voices.

'Where will I go?' Hagurosan asked.

'Follow the path,' the voice that was all voices said. '**You will find your way. And, Hagurosan**,' it added as he turned to leave, '**childhood is the purest state. The pure of heart never leave it behind. Their life merely takes them on a circuitous route away from, and then back to it**.'

Hagurosan didn't understand, but he sensed that the voice that was all voices had finished. He bowed once to the statue at the centre of the shrine, gazed one last time upon his mortal face (he hadn't realised he was *that* wrinkly!), then left the shrine at a quick pace, eager to see what the world was like.

Hagurosan descended the Holy Mountain at a brisk trot, no longer aware of the ravages of old age. He passed through an incredible, sprawling, modern town, unrecognisable as the village where he had lived. What impressed him most wasn't the new-style buildings, the fine roads, schools and playgrounds, but the look of joy and contentment on the faces of the people. They were no wealthier than those of most other towns, since all the money Hagurosan raised had gone towards the welfare of the children. But they were richer in spirit, and Hagurosan could now see that that was the greatest wealth of all.

As he left the town, the path and countryside changed, and he found himself in a new world, much like the one he had left, but brighter and lighter. He sensed that this world could be as peaceful or invigorating as he wished it to be, loud or quiet, vast or secluded. If, one day, the people of his world found the perfection he believed they were capable of enjoying, it would be just like this, and then perhaps there would be no need for two worlds, and people of all times and places could live together as one.

As Hagurosan walked, he felt his body change from that of an elderly man to that of a child. It was a rapid transformation, altering him in less than the blink of an eye. He stood, staring down at his tiny blemish-free hands and small crooked feet. Then someone shouted his name. A young girl was racing towards him, laughing and clapping. Other children followed, boys and girls, all as delighted as the girl in front.

Hagurosan was confused for just an instant. Then he realised who the girl was – his mother. And behind her, his father and other relatives, and friends from both his youth and old age. All were familiar, even though all were now children.

As Hagurosan's mother embraced him, and the other children surrounded him, he was filled with the understanding of this new world. It was no more than the voice that was all voices had told him. Childhood is the purest state, and the pure of heart always return to it. Life might be hard, and one might suffer with one's trials. But always, at the end, lay the promise of childhood's magic. For those who endured, the reward was a world of wonder, where every day was an adventure and every night a tableau of splendid, endless dreams.

Once he understood, Hagurosan laughed and hugged the children around him with renewed delight. He had lost nothing during his years in the shrine, or missed out on anything. The spirits had not cheated him of his childhood. Nobody could be cheated of childhood, not in the long run.

Hagurosan's band of friends and family broke apart after a while and drifted away. They would speak individually with Hagurosan later. They did not need to overwhelm him. There was no rush in this world. Hagurosan's mother squeezed his hand tightly and smiled. 'Are you ready for this?' she asked.

'Yes,' he said.

'Then let's go!' she whooped and ran with Hagurosan down to where the multitudes of children were playing and would continue to play, in peace, security and love, for all the circles of time and the endless loops beyond.

EOIN COLFER

mary's hair

ILLUSTRATION BY GRIFF

I hate my hair. Mammy says you shouldn't hate anything, but I can't help it. I hate my hair!

Just look at it! All bits. Brown bits, black bits, curly bits and straight bits. It looks like a big bush growing on top of my head. I wouldn't be surprised if I woke up one spring morning to find a family of swallows nesting in my bushy hair.

It's not fair. Other girls have lovely blonde hair. The kind you can put into pigtails. I tried to put my horrible hair into pigtails once, and the elastic bands snapped in the middle of playtime. My hair popped out, bushier than ever. Imelda, my best friend, thought my head was exploding.

Daddy says that if you don't like something, then you should do something about it, instead of just whingeing at your parents when they're trying to have a cup of tea. So, one day, that's what I decided to do. I decided to cut my hair until it looked the way I wanted it to. Just like those girls in the magazines.

I collected everything I needed, and made a little pile on my dressing table: scissors from the kitchen drawer, a tub of my brother's hair gel to flatten the curly bits, and a pair of swimming goggles to protect my eyes in case the scissors slipped.

First I put on the hair gel. It felt cold and gooey, like a family of snails crawling over my head, but at least it helped the goggles slide on smoothly. I probably should have washed those goggles before putting them on. There was all sorts of stuff inside the lenses. Sand from the beach, a blob of pink chewing gum, and a dried-up old starfish.

Then it was time to cut. The scissors felt funny in my fingers, pointing out instead of in. But there was no time to worry about that, Mammy could come in the door any second. So, I set to work. Slowly at first, just cutting one hair at a time. But when I realised how brilliant I was at hairdressing, I started snipping as fast as I could. Soon there were hundreds of curls on the bedroom carpet, like autumn leaves on the grass.

I took off the goggles. My hair looked absolutely brilliant. That was the last time the hairdresser got any money from me. Maybe I'd open a hairdresser's myself. In the bedroom. Mary's Hair, I'd call it. Ten pence a go, bring your own goggles.

Nearly all my curls were gone, just a few baby ones that I couldn't cut because the kitchen scissors were a bit blunt. I gave myself a fringe too. Very fashionable. It was a little bit crooked, but you'd hardly notice if I walked around with my head to one side.

I didn't know why I was worried at all. Mammy wouldn't be one bit cross. She'd probably be delighted that I'd saved her some money.

It was time to try out my new hairdo. All the girls would be playing at Imelda's, because Saturday was Barbie Day and Imelda's daddy just bought her the biggest doll's house in the shop.

I crept downstairs, making sure to keep my head to one side because of the fringe. I needn't have bothered creeping. Mammy and Daddy were far too busy trying to get baby Peter to open his mouth for some porridge to notice me. I don't blame Petey. I never liked porridge either.

Imelda lived two doors down. Usually I'd go through a hole in the hedges, but that day I went on the path, to protect my hairdo from grabby branches.

Imelda's mammy, Gloria, was in the front window polishing a vase. I gave her a big wave, and pointed to my head. Gloria was so impressed that she dropped the vase. You couldn't blame her.

She probably thought that I was one of those famous supermodels.

I could hear the girls round the back. They were all oohing and aahing and saying how great Imelda's doll's house was. Wait until they saw my hair!

I crept up behind the shrubs, then hopped out right in front of the girls.

'Here I am ladies!' I shouted. 'What do you think of me?'

No one said anything. I don't think they recognised me for a few seconds. Then the nicest thing happened. The girls started clapping. A round of applause, just for me. You'd swear I was a popstar or something. It was the happiest moment of my life. I decided I'd better make a speech.

'You're too kind, girls. You'd think I was after winning an Oscar. I'd just like to thank my mother for buying the scissors, and my big brother for leaving his door open, so I could borrow the hair gel. And, of course, all my friends for giving me the courage to cut my own hair.'

Imelda gave me a big hug, and a loan of Rollerblade Barbie. Only Imelda's best best friend got Rollerblade Barbie. We played for ages. We played Barbie goes to school, Barbie saves the ozone layer, and Barbie wins the world-wrestling title. It was brilliant.

After a while, I noticed that the girls were looking at my head. 'Nice, isn't it,' I said. 'It's hard to believe that it's all my own work.'

Imelda shook her head. 'It's not nice any more, Mary. The gel is drying out.'

I reached up with my fingers. The curls were back. The gel felt different too. Not slimy any more. Hard as a helmet. I got a funny feeling in my stomach. The kind you get just before a nasty shock. I dropped Rollerblade Barbie and picked up her vanity mirror. 'Oh no,' I said, the smile dropping off my face. My horrible bushy hair was back. Except now it was worse. My fringe had shrunk right up to the top of my forehead, and my curls looked like a million little horns.

Next thing I knew my mammy was standing in front of me. She'd just come in for a gossip with Gloria, and spotted me sitting in the garden.

'Mary!' she bawled. 'What have you done?'

I thought about blaming someone else for a minute. But there was no one. Even Petey had an alibi.

'You cut your hair, didn't you?'

I nodded. Too scared to speak.

'Look at the state of you. Well I hope you've learned your lesson.'

I nodded again. All the girls nodded along with me, just in case they were in trouble too.

'Get home now in front of me. Wait until your father sees this.'

I started crying then, big fat tears that dripped off the tip of my nose. It's a terrible thing to be popular for half an hour, and then have to go back to being plain old Mary Leary. I'd probably never get Rollerblade Barbie again.

* * *

I'd learned my lesson all right. I'd learned that if you're going to do something to your hair, it's a good idea to practise on someone else first. So I would have to find a volunteer for my hair experiments.

Mam made me promise never to cut my hair again. She even made sure that my fingers weren't crossed when I was making the promise. But she never said that I couldn't *dye* my hair. So that was what I decided to do next. If my hair was a lovely blonde colour, you might not notice the crooked fringe and the spiky curls.

The next morning I went looking for a volunteer to test the dye on. I asked the girls, but they ran away screaming, which usually means no. So I had to ask someone who would do absolutely anything just to have a friend.

Noely Rochford always had a runny nose. By the age of seven he still hadn't figured out how to use a hanky. This meant that not even the other boys, who were a fairly smelly bunch themselves, wanted to hang around with him. So when I called at Noely's house that Sunday, he was fairly surprised to see me.

Noely answered the door wearing a woolly hat, Pooh pyjamas and fuzzy bunny slippers.

'How would you like a friend?' I said.

'Who is it?'

'Me. Only for today though.'

Noely thought about it for a second, wiping his nose on his pyjama sleeve.

'OK.'

'There's one condition though. You'll have to get your hair dyed blonde.'

Noely wiped his nose on the other sleeve.

'OK.'

'Come on then. The hairdresser's is in my house. I'll sit on the wall until you get changed.'

'Changed?'

Boys, honestly, they've no brains.

'Into your clothes, Noely. You can't wear your pyjamas through the estates.'

'Oh. OK.'

It took Noely nearly an hour to get changed. My bum was getting sore sitting on that wall. I was thinking about looking for another volunteer, when the door opened and out he came.

'Oh no!' I moaned. Noely had taken his hat off, and there was hardly any hair on his head.

'I got a shave,' he said. 'A number two. Do you like it?'

'No, Noely, I don't like it. How am I supposed to dye a bald head?' I thought he was going to cry then.

'Are you not my friend any more?'

I nearly said no. But then I remembered something.

'Noely. Don't you have a dog? A little shaggy-haired dog?'

'Yep,' said Noely. 'Bruce is my best friend in the world.'

'Hmm,' I said, thinking of another brilliant idea. 'Why don't you ask him to come with us.'

* * *

My brilliant idea was to dye the dog's hair. If the whole experiment went wrong, Bruce wouldn't even be able to complain, except to other dogs.

I sneaked Noely and Bruce upstairs to the bathroom. I needn't have bothered sneaking. Mammy and Daddy were busy trying to stop Petey kicking long enough to change his nappy.

Bruce was perfect for my experiment. He had a big head of shaggy brown hair. Nearly exactly like mine. Now all I had to do was get Bruce into the shower. The instructions on the packet of hair dye were simple: wet hair and rub in solution. No problem.

I gave Noely his orders.

'Tell Bruce to get into the bath. You get in with him and hold his head still.'

Noely sniffed. 'Can't.'

'And why not, Mister Rochford?' The teacher always called Noely Mister when she was annoyed with him.

'I'm not allowed in the bath without my mammy, Teacher... I mean Mary.'

'Well how am I supposed to wet Bruce's hair then? And what's he doing now?'

Bruce had his head stuck down the toilet. His hind legs were up on the toilet seat.

'He's having a drink. Bruce loves drinking out of the toilet.'

And suddenly I had another brilliant idea. I tiptoed over to the toilet, and lifted off the cistern lid. It was really heavy, but I'm very strong for my size.

The water inside was blue, because of the toilet bleach, but I thought it should be OK for my experiment. I poured in all the hair dye, and stirred it around with Daddy's toothbrush. Then I flushed the toilet!

Whoosh went the water, all over Bruce's head. The poor chap fell right into the bowl, spinning round and round with the blue water.

Noely started crying. 'Bruce is drowning! What have you done, Mary Leary?'

Maybe my idea wasn't so brilliant after all.

But then the toilet stopped flushing, and Bruce's head popped up over the rim.

'Ruff,' said Bruce. And it wasn't a happy ruff. It was an *I'll-get-you for that* ruff. He hopped out of the toilet and ran off down the stairs.

Noely wiped his nose with a finger, then he pointed the finger at me. 'I'm telling on you, Mary Leary. And I'm not your friend any more either.'

Noely ran off after his dog. I didn't understand why Bruce was so upset. It was only a bit of hair dye and some bleach. Now I couldn't even check the results of my experiment.

I was putting Daddy's toothbrush back when I noticed something. All the bristles were gone. They had melted away. Now what could have done that?

Mammy made me go and say sorry to Noely. He was still crying even after two days.

'Sorry Noely,' I said, trying to sound really sad.

'You made Bruce all funny looking, Mary Leary.'

It was true. Bruce did look funny. Half his body was white, and the other half was brown. He looked like two dogs stuck together.

'I think he looks nice. Like a superhero dog.'

'Really?'

'Really. Do you forgive me now?'

'No. And Bruce doesn't either.'

That was a surprise. I was expecting Noely to forgive me straight away, just to have a friend.

'Friends forgive each other,' I said.

Noely lifted his sleeve to wipe his nose. There was a plaster on the sleeve. There was a message written on the plaster. It said: *Use your hanky*. Noely took a hanky from his pocket and gave his nose a big blow.

'You're not my real friend. You only wanted to play so you could turn Bruce white. Bruce is my real friend.'

Noely was right. Bruce was his real friend. I'd only called at his house because none of the girls would let me dye their hair.

'If I play with you for a week, will you forgive me then?'

Noely thought about it. 'A month.'

'Two weeks.'

'OK,' he said. 'It's a deal.'

We shook hands, because that's what you do when you make a deal. Noely's hand was a bit sticky. I heard Mammy calling me from up the street.

'I have to go now,' I said.

'Where?'

'Mammy's taking me to have my hair cut. Really short so it'll grow out evenly.'

'A skinner?'

I nodded. I didn't want a skinner. I hadn't had short hair since I was a baby.

Noely smiled. 'Well don't worry, Mary. Even if your hair turns out horrible, I'll still play with you.'

'Thanks, Noely. You're a real friend.'

I ran up the road. Mammy was beeping the car horn for me to hurry up. Maybe Noely wouldn't be such a bad friend after all. He had a cool dog, and he was good at taking orders. The most important thing was that he was learning to use a handkerchief.

No more tricks. Real friends didn't play tricks. Anyway Mammy had banned me from using hair dye. So now I couldn't cut or dye my hair. But Mammy hadn't said anything about perms. Maybe I could give myself one of those.

ANNIE DALTON

angels' night off

ILLUSTRATION BY RIAN HUGHES

I don't mean to sound bigheaded, but if the kids at my old Earth comprehensive could see me now, they would definitely be amazed. They just would NOT believe that Mel Beeby, style-princess and well-known ditz, could win a major celestial scholarship to study at the Angel Academy!

OK, so I had to die to get here, which was a little harsh. I was only thirteen at the time. But my new school has to be the best school in the entire cosmos. The campus is situated right on the edge of the most vibey district of the Heavenly City. There's SO much to do here, it's unbelievable.

Unfortunately, for the past few weeks I haven't had time to do more than snatch the occasional snack at my fave student hangout. That's because I've been hurrying through the streets in a total blur on my way to, or from, yet another long shift at the Angel Watch centre.

A hideous war had started up in the first decade of the twenty-first century. The Agency had been keeping close watch on the situation and already sent in teams of highly trained celestial agents.

Then one night, my best mate Lola and I were listening to a late night heavenly radio station, when an urgent appeal went out for volunteers to help out at the Angel Watch centre.

Lollie and I hurried down right away. We're both originally from Earth, so basically anything that affects that little blue-green planet affects us.

Dozens of concerned angel trainees were going in through the revolving doors. Three other girls from our dorm – Amber, Meena and Kwan Yin – had come rushing across town in their PJs. Like us, they'd heard the appeal and sprinted down to help.

The Angel Watch centre is vast. It takes up an entire floor of the Agency tower, that's kind of Angel HQ. Lola and I managed to find empty booths next to each other. We kicked off our shoes (sending vibes is easier in bare feet), logged on to our computers, and began working our way down long lists of names.

Divine computers are way more advanced than the human kind. We'd type in a name, then a live picture flashed up on the screen, and we'd see and hear our human child, wherever they happened to be in the war zone. We'd also get screeds of highly technical angelic info, letting us know exactly what kind of vibes to send and for how long.

I know what you're thinking. These kids were in acute physical danger. Their extremely poor country was currently being bombed into rubble by enemy planes. They needed shelter, food, medicines and clean water. Shouldn't our agents be airlifting these kids to safety? What use are airy-fairy vibes in such a drastic situation?

I used to ask myself exactly these kinds of questions. But I've been a trainee angel for a few terms now, and I've found out that there's far more at stake than humans realise.

Here are three very good reasons why angels are not allowed to save you from yourselves.

1. Humans have free will. That means angels mustn't interfere even when humans are acting like inmates of some vast insane asylum.

2. If we constantly rushed to the rescue, you'd never evolve to the next stage. You'd never ever figure out who you really are.

3. Also, if angels solved all your problems for you, you'd never understand how this incredibly magical universe actually works.

Still confused? OK, I'll try to explain.

To humans, the universe seems like a solid, reliable environment, filled with solid reliable phenomena: trees, superstores, tower blocks, etc. Stuff you can measure and weigh or even blow up with bombs. But to angels, the universe isn't solid at all. It's pure energy that is merely disguised as trees and tower blocks. Far from being airy-fairy, vibes are what the universe is made from! Isn't that AMAZING? *You* are made out of the exact same stuff as the stars and planets!!

I'm going to tell you something else that's going to shock your socks off. Want to know WHY this universe was created?

So we could all have fun!

I know, NOW we tell you! Don't worry, the idea of the cosmos as some huge heavenly playground still strikes me as totally far-fetched, too. But our big buddy Reuben, who has never lived on Earth, swears it's true. He says cosmic energy is basically a fabulously advanced play material. He says once you get the hang of a few simple laws, you'll realise you can do anything you want with it. Unfortunately, humans are taking aeons to figure this out. In the process, a lot of you guys are getting hurt.

The good news is you're not in this alone. Bringing peace to Planet Earth is probably the biggest and most demanding project the Agency has ever undertaken. There are celestial personnel stationed in every single century of human history, all doing their bit to help humans get the message. Plus we've got some of you on Angel Watch twenty-four-seven.

We don't just support victims of wars and catastrophes, incidentally. We also target kids in Earth's more fortunate areas. OK, so their houses aren't being bombed and they don't have to cross minefields to fetch clean water. They've also got more than enough to eat, but that doesn't necessarily mean they're happy. Kids in rich countries are often anything but. Plus, they easily get confused.

What with shopping malls and TV, (not to mention constant brainwashing from the Powers of Darkness), they tend to forget how magical they are. They forget they're actually undercover angels on a mission to make Earth a better place. I know I did!

That's why we keep giving you friendly cosmic nudges, encouraging you to notice what you're doing to yourselves and all the other life forms on your beautiful planet. We want you to remember that it's up to YOU to make a difference.

But you knew that already right? That's why you're reading this book. So I know you'll understand when I say that being an angel has to be the most rewarding job in the universe. But it's also incredibly intense. After a few weeks, going to school by day and working down at Angel Watch by night, my mates and I were getting totally drained. Without knowing it, we were gradually slipping into that numb frame of mind, where it almost seems like human violence and cruelty is all there is.

One morning we were all slumped at a table in our favourite café in a state of total exhaustion. Lola could hardly even move her lips. 'Just look at us,' she mumbled. 'We're supposed to be vibrant immortal beings and we're burned out wrecks!'

'We've got to do something,' Kwan Yin agreed.

Meena had humungous dark shadows under her eyes, 'A teacher told me when angels get this low, it's because they're taking life too seriously,' she yawned.

This made me see red. 'Hello! I've just spent an hour watching this little orphaned boy sitting on a heap of rubble that used to be his house. I don't see how it's possible to take that too seriously, do you!'

Meena scowled. 'I'm only telling you what he said!'

'Meena's teacher was right,' said Lola unexpectedly. 'We can't go on like this. We need to do something for US for a change. Something fun.'

'Like what?' I said in a dull voice.

'Hey, don't make me group leader!' Lola objected. 'I'm tired too, you know.'

We all went back into our slump.

'What did you guys do in *your* time that was fun?' Amber asked me.

'Loads of things: shopping, clubbing, watched horror videos...'

'Ugh, horror videos, no thanks,' shuddered Lola.

I had a reviving sip of my smoothie. 'Sometimes we had sleepovers.'

Lola sat up. 'Sleepovers?'

'You probably didn't have those in your century. A sleepover's when your mates come over and stay the night, you play silly games—'

'—tell stories, try out each other's make-up,' Lola finished.

I blinked at her. 'You had sleepovers in the twenty-second century?'

'With four brothers? Are you crazy! But I slept over at my friends' houses all the time.'

'Did you make your special hot chocolate?' I asked enviously.

Lola grinned. 'Is my name Lola Sanchez?!'

'Let's do it,' said Meena excitedly. 'Let's have a – what do you call it? – a sleepout.'

'It wouldn't work,' I objected. 'Our rooms are way too small.'

'So? We'll sleep out on the beach!' Amber's tired face was suddenly shining. 'We can bring food. I'll make brownies.'

'Let's do it tonight!' said Lola.

'We can't. We're due down at the Angel Watch centre,' I reminded them.

'Mel, we've been there every night for almost a month,' said Lola. 'I'm sorry, but even an angel deserves a night off.'

'I don't know,' I said anxiously. 'The Agency are so short-staffed and those kids are in a bad way. They really need us, Lollie.'

The other girls eventually talked me round. To be honest, I didn't put up much of a fight. I was too knackered.

That night, instead of spending the night staring at distressing images of children on a computer screen, the five of us walked down to a deserted heavenly cove.

It was a warm night and stars sparkled in the night sky like big spangly sequins. Pure white sands stretched away as far as we could see, and the waves made soothing sounds as they washed in and out.

We went hunting for driftwood and had a fire crackling away in no time. Amber happily toasted marshmallows over the blaze. Meena started painting cosmic patterns on Lola's hands, with some henna she'd brought along especially.

'Aah,' breathed Lola. 'This is more like it!'

But I couldn't get that little boy out of my head. He'd been sitting all by himself in the ruins. He was so shocked he couldn't even cry.

Lola often reads my mind. 'It's just one night,' she said softly.

'Come and swim,' suggested Kwan Yin. 'It'll do you good.' She grabbed my hand, pulling me with her, down to the sea.

I love swimming in Heaven. Fishes come right up to you, and the ocean is silky and warm, and somehow alive. I could actually feel the sea water washing my worries away.

By the time we got out, Lola had brewed up a big pot of her special hot chocolate. I sat by the fire, warming my hands round my mug, inhaling sea-salt and wood-smoke smells. The cinnamon-scented fumes were wafting from my hot chocolate and, to my amazement, I felt something I hadn't felt for weeks. Total peace.

'You never told me you guys were having a party!'

Our buddy Reuben stood beaming at us, twiddling one of his tiny dreads. As a pure angel, Reubs doesn't need to sleep, so he often goes out for a midnight stroll. Normally I'd be delighted to see him, but I felt deeply embarrassed. On Earth, sleepovers are strictly a girl thing.

'No problem,' he said quickly, when I awkwardly explained the situation. 'Have a great time,' and he turned to go.

We all exchanged anxious glances.

'Did you see his face?' I hissed. 'I feel SO mean.'

'Couldn't he be like, our guest?' suggested Kwan Yin.

'Great idea,' Lola agreed. 'Yo! DJ Sweetpea!' she called. 'Come back! We'd like you to stay.'

Meena gave a chuckle. 'Actually, we'd like you to tell your friends!'

'And bring a sound system!' Lola added, laughing. 'These angels are ready to bop till they drop!'

News of our beach party spread like wildfire. Half the people who turned up, we didn't even know! A pair of decks magically materialised from somewhere, and our buddy Reuben, a.k.a. DJ Sweetpea, got right into the mix, with his unique fusion of earthly and heavenly sounds.

Out of all Reuben's songs, my favourite has to be *You're Not Alone*. Towards the end of the night, the familiar bass line came floating across the sand and everyone joined in. 'We're not alone!' we all sang blissfully over and over. 'We're not alone!'

Then I gave a gasp of surprise. I could see our energy fields!

When angels send vibes, we get strange tingling sensations in our hands and hearts. A couple of times I'd glimpsed vague swirls of colour around my mates, but I'd told myself I was imagining it. But these pulsing patterns of light were definitely not imaginary. Vibrant, gorgeous colours flowed from our hearts and hands, pouring out into the dark.

I found myself remembering a cheesy car sticker I once saw on Earth.

It said, '*Angels fly because they take themselves lightly.*'

The thing about cheesy statements is they're often true. I'd let myself become seriously bogged down in human suffering. Then my sensible mates made me lighten up. Now, totally without the aid of Heavenly technology, without even any effort, our energy was beaming down to Earth, going exactly where it was most needed

I pictured the lonely kids in shopping malls who had forgotten they were magic, and the little boy in the rubble, so numb he couldn't cry.

'You're not alone,' I told them softly. 'We're with you for as long as it takes.'

I wrapped my arms around my knees, and watched as the shimmering unearthly colours streamed away into the night. I carried on watching, until the sun came up over the rim of the sea and a new day began in Heaven.

PS I asked my mates for the recipes for their sleepover goodies in case you want to try them out.

HEAVENLY HOT CHOCOLATE

Lola makes this by melting wickedly delicious twenty-second century chocolate bars. But don't worry, the twenty-first century kind is fine. The good news is you can make it in the microwave and it still tastes totally sublime!

600ml / 1 pint milk
150g/5oz your favourite chocolate, chopped
ground cinnamon
sugar
mini marshmallows
whipped cream

Put the milk into a microwave-safe container and cook on HIGH for 2 minutes. Mix in the chocolate and ½ teaspoon of cinnamon. Return to the microwave and cook on HIGH for 2 to 3 minutes or until the chocolate has completely melted (be careful not to let it boil over). Whisk until smooth and frothy and pour into 3 mugs. Add sugar if needed. Decorate with whipped cream, a dusting of cinnamon and cute mini-marshmallows.

AMBER'S SUGAR SHOCK BROWNIES

When these are ready, you should cut them into very small pieces otherwise humans will get serious sugar shock!!

For the Brownies
125g/4oz dark chocolate, chopped
225g/8oz unsalted butter
450g/1lb sugar4 eggs125g/4oz plain flour
50g/2oz chopped walnuts
2 tsp vanilla essence

Preheat oven to 180°C / 350°F / Gas Mark 4. Line a 32cm x 23cm/13" x 9" tin making sure the paper overlaps the edges by at least three inches on all sides – this mixture rises!

Melt the chocolate and butter in a heavy saucepan over a low heat, stirring until smooth. Let it cool for 15 minutes. Beat the sugar and eggs in a large bowl until light and fluffy. Gradually stir in the chocolate mixture. Add the flour, half the walnuts and vanilla essence and stir until combined. Spread the brownie batter into your prepared tin and bake for 40-50 minutes until set.

Prepare the Fudge Topping while brownies are baking.

For the Brownie Fudge Topping
1kg/2lb4oz sugar
75g/2.5oz butter
410g can evaporated milk
3 x 100g bag plain chocolate chips
2 tsp vanilla essence
50g/2oz chopped walnuts

Combine the sugar, butter and milk in a large saucepan. Bring to the boil over a medium heat, stirring constantly. Boil for 6 minutes, stirring constantly (this mixture burns easily, so be sure to keep stirring!). Remove from the heat and add the chocolate chips and the vanilla essence. Beat until smooth. Stir in the walnuts.

Remove the brownies from the oven when done and immediately pour the Fudge Topping over them. Cool in the pan on a wire rack, then place in the freezer until firm, about 1 hour. Cut into 3cm / 1" squares to serve. Store the uneaten brownies in the fridge.

EASIEST FUDGE IN THE UNIVERSE

Cooking is totally not my thing, so when I have to make food for a party, I just make this fudge. It really is the easiest recipe ever!

300g (3 x 100g bag) chocolate chips
405g can condensed milk

Place the chocolate chips and milk in a microwave-safe bowl. Place in the microwave on medium power for 2-3 minutes, stirring after 2 minutes. Keep in the microwave, stirring at 1 minute intervals, until the chips are melted and the mixture is smooth and thick. If you don't have a microwave, you can melt the chips and milk in a heavy saucepan over low heat.

Pour into a lined 20cm / 8"square tin and cool.

ENJOY!

PPS Don't forget to ask for help if you need it, things can get very HOT in the kitchen!

GARTH NIX
charlie rabbit

Abbas woke to the scream of sirens. Half-asleep, he tumbled out of the upper bunk, and shook his brother who was asleep below.

'Joshua! Get up!'

Joshua opened one eye, but he didn't move any other muscle. He was six, and unruly. Abbas, who was eleven, felt practically grown-up by comparison.

'I don't want to go down the hole,' complained Joshua. He still hadn't opened his other eye.

Abbas pulled the bedclothes back and dragged Joshua on to the floor. Charlie Rabbit, who had been under the blankets, fell out too. His long floppy ears sprawled across Abbas's bare feet, till Joshua grabbed his constant companion and hugged him to his chest.

'It's a cellar, not a hole, and we have to go now!'

Joshua lay on the floor and shut both eyes. Abbas hauled him up into a sitting position, but Joshua was as floppy as Charlie Rabbit's ears. As soon as Abbas let go, Joshua slumped down again.

'Mum!' shouted Abbas, a touch of panic in his voice. He could feel a rapid, regular vibration through the walls and floor, and could hear something like distant thunder beneath the shrieking sirens. But it wasn't thunder. The cruise missiles were hitting the south side. The next wave would strike much closer to home. He had to get Joshua to the shelter.

'Mum!'

There was no answer. Abbas, still half-asleep, felt a sudden pain of memory. Their mother had been wounded in a daylight air raid that afternoon, and had been taken away. To a hospital, Abbas desperately hoped, if there was one left. His grandparents were supposed to come over, but they hadn't arrived by nightfall. Abbas had put Joshua to bed and then, much later, had fallen into an exhausted sleep himself.

He tried not to think about what might have happened to Grandpa and Gramma, in the same way he tried not to think about his father, who had been drafted eighteen months before. The single postcard they had got from him was still pinned to the wall of their room, its edges curled, the ink fading.

No one could help him, Abbas realised. He had to look after Joshua by himself.

'You stay, then!' Abbas shouted. He snatched Charlie Rabbit from Joshua and ran to the door. 'Charlie Rabbit will come with me.'

'Wait!' squealed Joshua. He jumped up and reached for his rabbit. But Abbas held it above his head, and ran for the stairs. Joshua followed, pleading and clutching at his brother's pyjamas to make him stop. Somehow, they made it down the stairs together, without Abbas losing his pyjamas or his temper.

The cellar was entered through a trapdoor in the kitchen that led to a long, narrow ladder. As Abbas flung the trapdoor open, there was a terrible booming crash outside. The whole house shook and a storm of dust and pieces of plaster rained down from the ceiling. The light near the stove sparked and went out, leaving them in darkness. Joshua lost his balance and fell over, almost rolling into the trapdoor. Purely by luck, Abbas got in the way, and they lay tangled together on the floor.

'Down the ladder!' shouted Abbas, as Joshua started to howl. He wrestled the little boy around and lowered him down by feel.

'Charleeee! Charleeee!' screamed Joshua. He hung on to the ladder with one hand while he clawed at Abbas with the other, trying to grab Charlie Rabbit.

'Charlie's coming too! Climb down! Down!'

Another missile hit nearby. Abbas felt the impact through his whole body. It took a moment for him to realise that it had knocked him senseless for a few seconds. He was still on the kitchen floor, but he couldn't feel the trapdoor – or Joshua. He couldn't hear anything either, because it felt like a school bell was going off deep inside his ears.

Blinded and deafened, he was so disoriented it took several seconds of panicked reaching around before he realised he was backed up against the fridge. That meant the trapdoor should be over to the right. He crawled in that direction, and felt his probing fingers drop into the open trapdoor. But where was Joshua?

There was an electric lantern at the foot of the ladder. Abbas realised he had to get it before he could look for Joshua. He lowered himself through the trapdoor as another missile hit nearby. This time Abbas saw the flash, which meant the blackout curtains over the windows were gone. Or perhaps the whole wall had fallen over. Hastily he stepped down, dragging the trapdoor shut behind him, though it did little to muffle the sound of explosions.

Abbas's hearing started to come back before he reached the foot of the ladder. A distant, piercing voice penetrated his aching ears. Joshua's voice.

'It's dark! Where's Charlie? Charlie!'

'Stay still!' instructed Abbas, far too loudly, since he couldn't hear himself. 'I'll find Charlie after I get the light.'

He felt around behind the ladder. The emergency box was there, and the large electric lantern they used to take camping. Years ago, when there were still holidays and you could leave the city without a special pass.

Abbas switched the lantern on. Nothing happened, and a sob began to rise in the boy's throat. They had saved those batteries especially, kept them for exactly this sort of emergency. They couldn't have gone flat...

A faint glow appeared before the sob could leave Abbas's mouth, and slowly grew till it became a bright, white light. Abbas turned the sob into a cough and looked around. Joshua was already picking up Charlie Rabbit. The little boy was dirty, but otherwise seemed unhurt, though he must have fallen halfway down the ladder.

'Nothing hurts?' asked Abbas.

Joshua shook his head and hid his face in Charlie Rabbit's ears.

Abbas looked around. The 'hole' had been an ice cellar, long ago, and was really only a cave dug into the thick clay below the house. Where the ice blocks had once been stacked, there was now a makeshift shelter, an A-frame made from two heavy tabletops with the legs cut off, bolted together at the top and sandbagged at the bottom and each end.

Another missile exploded close by, the ground shivering from the impact. More dust fell from the ceiling.

'Into... the shelter,' gasped Abbas, as he pushed his brother towards the wooden A-frame. For once, Joshua did as he was told, even taking the lantern from Abbas, who turned back and picked up the heavy emergency box. It contained a couple of old blankets, some food and a bottle of water.

Abbas had taken only two steps towards the shelter when a cruise missile hit the house next door. The explosion shattered the whole street, smashing every house like a sledgehammer coming down on matchstick models.

The earth under Abbas's feet rolled and all the air around him was sucked up with a terrible scream. He was lifted up, then thrown forward, almost to the shelter. He landed hard, on his side, but had no time to think about the pain. The scream of air dissipated, but in its place came a terrible groaning noise, an almost human expression of pain, though it was far louder than any human sound.

It was the house. Abbas looked up and saw the floor above bulge down, every beam protesting under a terrible strain. The whole building was about to collapse.

Without hesitation, Abbas threw the emergency box towards the shelter and flung himself after it, an instant before the space where he'd been was hit by a huge roof beam.

As the beam fell, the floor above gave way and the ruins of the house came pouring down, a great dumping of broken wooden beams, floor planks, plaster, roof tiles and chimney bricks, mixed in with furniture, books, even the bath.

The wooden walls of the shelter boomed and shook as the cascade of ruin continued. Abbas pushed Joshua right to the back as debris began to flow in through the shelter entrance, preceded by a thick wave of dust; cloying, sticky dust that made it almost impossible to breathe and dimmed the light of the lantern.

Joshua screamed as debris continued to crash down. Abbas was about to tell him to shut up, when he realised he was screaming too. Abbas forced himself to stop, shutting the scream inside as he crawled to the far end of the shelter, dragging his little brother and Charlie Rabbit with him.

Joshua's screaming became a choking sob as the sound of the falling debris diminished. Abbas kept holding him, as much for his own comfort as his brother's. Both of them jumped and shivered every time the shelter was hit by something particularly large. Would it hold? Could it hold?

It did hold. Eventually the crashing descent of debris stopped.

A little more spread in through the entrance, but there were no more terrifying booms and thuds upon the shelter.

Joshua's sobs slowed. He coughed and mumbled a few words. It took Abbas a few seconds to work out that he'd asked, 'Are we dead?'

'No, we're...' began Abbas. He had to stop and cough before starting again. There was so much dust that he could barely breathe, let alone talk.

'Not dead!' he gasped. 'Don't move. I'll... get water.'

He crawled across to the emergency box, which was buried in bits of broken wood and plaster rubble, but Abbas managed to dig through and retrieve it. Beyond the box, the entrance to the shelter was completely blocked with debris. There was no way out.

Abbas tried to open the water bottle but his hands were shaking too much. He put the bottle between his knees and tried again, and managed to unscrew the cap. He took a cautious swallow and spat out a mouthful of muddy dust. Then he held the bottle for Joshua, making sure his brother could not drink too much or spill it.

'More!' demanded Joshua.

Abbas shook his head and screwed the lid tight.

'No more for now,' he said quietly. 'Later.'

Joshua's lower lip trembled but he didn't protest. He just held Charlie Rabbit tighter, his small face crumpled in shock and puzzlement.

Abbas wiped the dust off the lantern. The light brightened, but that didn't help. It lit up a tiny pocket of clear space, just big enough for the two of them to crouch in.

They were completely buried under the ruins of the house.

From the continuing tremble he could feel through the floor, Abbas knew that there were still missiles falling, though they were striking farther away. That meant there would be little or no chance of rescue. There were already thousands of destroyed houses. No one would search under this one. No one knew they would be here.

Joshua mumbled something, the words lost in Charlie Rabbit's ears.

'It's OK,' said Abbas. He wished he sounded more convincing. He cleared his throat and tried again. 'We're safe here, now.'

'Where's Mum?' said Joshua, more audibly. 'I want Mum.'

Abbas closed his eyes for a second. *I have to be brave. I have to be brave.*

'She's OK too. She'll... she'll come and get us in the morning.'

'When is it morning?'

'Not for a long time. Try to go back to sleep.'

Joshua stared at his brother.

'Can't sleep.'

'I'll tell you a story.'

'A Charlie Rabbit story?'

'Uh, I suppose. Let me try and remember the story for a second.'

Joshua nodded his agreement. He loved stories.

Abbas didn't try to think of a story. He tried to think about what they could do. He had to remember everything his father had told him about the shelter, about what to do. But it was over a year ago, and he hadn't paid attention—

'Who else is in the story?'

'What?'

'Who else is in the story, besides Charlie?'

Abbas shook his head. He couldn't think, but Joshua needed a story. He had to be distracted from their situation.

'There were two boys,' he said. 'Their names were—'

'Abbas and Joshua!'

'OK, Abbas and Joshua. They lived long ago in a city of white towers, in a beautiful and peaceful kingdom. Everyone was happy and there was plenty to eat and good things to drink, like hot chocolate. Abbas and Joshua went to a school which had lots of books and teachers for every subject. But one day a terrible giant appeared and demanded that everyone in the city hand over half their gold or—'

'He would eat them?'

'No... he would destroy their city. The giant was so big and so horrible that the people had no choice. Abbas and Joshua had no gold, but their parents had to give up half their life savings to the giant. The giant took the gold and went away and everyone was happy again.'

'Didn't they ask Charlie Rabbit for help?'

'No, not yet. They thought if they gave the gold the giant would go away. But the next year the giant came back again, and this time he had brought his friends. Three huge giants, who stamped and shouted and demanded all the gold that was left or they would smash the people into little pieces.'

'Why didn't they fight? I bet Abbas and Joshua would fight.'

'They couldn't fight. The giants were too big, and they could throw huge rocks from far away. So the people of the city handed over their gold and hoped that they would never see the giants again.'

'But the giants came back?'

'Yes, the giants came back. This time they didn't ask for gold. They said they were going to smash the city into little bits and there was nothing anyone could do about it—'

'Except Charlie Rabbit!'

'Yes, but no one knew where Charlie Rabbit was. He'd gone away and he hadn't come back.'

'But he did!'

'Well, first of all Abbas and Joshua decided to go looking for him. But before they could leave, the giants started to throw rocks at the city. Huge rocks, bigger than houses, that fell down from the sky, smashing everything to bits.

'Abbas and Joshua were in their house when the first rock struck. They knew they couldn't go out, so they climbed down a ladder into a cave. There was a secret tunnel from the cave, that came out beyond the city walls. But while they were still in the cave a really big rock hit directly above them!'

Joshua took a sharp intake of breath. His eyes were huge, staring at Abbas, waiting for what happened next.

'The cave collapsed all around the two boys. They were trapped.'

'What happened then?'

'Then...' Abbas began, but he couldn't go on. His mouth trembled and he felt tears start in his eyes. 'Then...'

'Then Charlie Rabbit came back,' said Joshua, eagerly taking over the story. 'Charlie Rabbit smelled the boys in the tunnel and he dugged them up. Then Charlie Rabbit jumped over to the giants and he kicked them with his big foots. Wham! Wham! Wham! Wham! Wham! The giants ran away and everyone was happy and Charlie Rabbit ate a carrot.'

Abbas nodded.

'Yes... that was what happened.'

'I'm going to sleep now,' announced Joshua. He dragged one of the old blankets out of the box and curled up on it. 'Wake me up when Charlie Rabbit comes to dig us out.'

'I will,' said Abbas. He felt so helpless. If only there was a secret tunnel, or a real Charlie Rabbit...

Secret tunnel. Another way out.

Abbas remembered what his father had said. There was another way out. The shelter backed on to the old ice chute, which had been used long ago to slide the ice blocks from the street down to the cellar.

Abbas took a deep breath, then coughed it away. There was

too much dust for deep breaths. Or maybe the air was running out. He took a shallower breath, and edged around Joshua to the back of the shelter. The wall there looked just like the hard clay of the other walls.

Abbas tapped it, and was rewarded with a hollow sound. He let out a sobbing half-laugh and started to scrape. There was a wooden hatch behind the clay, one so rotten that it crumbled at his touch. Abbas attacked it eagerly, pulling at the wood in a frenzy, ignoring the splinters.

There was a narrow chute beyond the hatch. Abbas crawled a little way up it, then looked back at Joshua, marvelling at his little brother's ability to sleep. Should he wake him? Or should he make sure the chute was clear all the way to the street?

Abbas hesitated, then edged back down. As he backed into the shelter again, he heard Joshua sit up. And there was another noise, something rustling in the debris. A sound he couldn't quite place.

'Abbas! It's wet!'

It took Abbas a second to turn around in the confined space. By the time he could see, he could already feel the water around his ankles. It was freezing cold, and rising very quickly.

Broken water pipe. Maybe a big one. A water main. We have to get out!

'It's OK, Josh,' Abbas said quickly. He picked up the lantern and showed Joshua the entrance. 'I've found the tunnel. The secret tunnel. You go up first. Quickly.'

Joshua scrambled up into the ice chute. Still sleepy, he didn't pick up Charlie Rabbit. Abbas started after him, but at the last moment grabbed the rabbit. Joshua would want it for sure, later.

Water burbled around Abbas's knees as he climbed up into the chute. It was rising very quickly, far too quickly. Abbas pushed at Joshua's legs to make him go faster.

'Hurry up!'

They crawled up at least ten metres, with the water always lapping at Abbas's feet, sometimes even catching up to his knees. Joshua's speed varied, and Abbas had to keep pushing at him.

Then Joshua stopped altogether and let out a howl of protest as Abbas shoved at his legs.

'What's wrong? Keep going!'

'Can't,' said Joshua.

Abbas shone the light up. He could see the top hatch. But it was broken and hanging down, and where the open air should be, there was a huge slab of concrete, its reinforcing wires hanging down like severed tree roots.

It was the roof of the bus shelter from across the street. It must have been blown off and come straight down on the ice chute exit. Now there really was no way out.

Abbas twisted around. The water was slowly swirling around his thighs. Cold, dark water, constantly rising.

'Lie on your side,' instructed Abbas. Joshua rolled over, and Abbas crawled up next to him. They could both just fit that way, though it was a squeeze. Charlie Rabbit was once again between them, and Joshua gratefully grabbed his ears.

Abbas worked the lantern around and shone it on the concrete slab that blocked their way. There was a small gap in one corner, not much larger than a softball. Abbas reached out and tried to crumble the concrete edges, but only made his fingers bleed.

'Can... can you fit through there?' Abbas asked his brother hopefully. The water was up to his knees again, despite the extra yards he'd gained by moving next to Joshua.

Joshua shook his head. The gap was far too small.

Abbas put his hand against the wall. He couldn't feel any explosions. The missile strike must be over. The civil defence teams would be out. But how could he attract their attention quickly enough? They'd be drowned in ten or twenty minutes.

'Help!' he shouted, the word leaping out of his mouth almost without him thinking about it. Joshua flinched at the noise. 'Help!'

The sound echoed back from the concrete and the rising water, but Abbas knew it had not penetrated above ground. No one could hear him.

'I'm cold,' whimpered Joshua. 'It's wet.'

'I'm trying to get help,' said Abbas. 'I'm trying—

'Charlie Rabbit—'

'Shut up about Charlie Rabbit!' screamed Abbas. He grabbed the rabbit and pulled its ears apart, trying to rip it in his desperate anger. 'Charlie Rabbit is a toy!'

Joshua started to sob again, deep, wracking sobs that shook his whole body.

Abbas stopped pulling Charlie Rabbit's ears and stared at its big-eyed, long-nosed, furry face. Charlie Rabbit was a toy. A very fancy toy.

'Ssshhh, it's OK,' Abbas said more gently. 'I'm sorry. Charlie Rabbit is going to help us.'

Joshua's sobs became a sniffle.

'He is?'

'He is,' confirmed Abbas. He tore off a long piece of wood from the broken hatch and propped it against the gap in the concrete block. Then he opened the panel on the back of Charlie Rabbit. 'Only we have to sit in the dark for a while, because Charlie needs the batteries from the lantern. Can you be brave for Charlie Rabbit?'

'Yes...'

Abbas set Charlie down between them, turned off the lantern and took out the carefully hoarded batteries one at a time.

One slip now, one battery dropped down the chute... I must concentrate... this has to work...

He got the batteries in, slid the switch to 'Maximum' and closed the panel. Would Charlie still work? Even if he did, would it help? The water was up to his waist now, and it was so cold he couldn't feel his legs any more.

'Joshua,' he whispered. 'Feel for Charlie. Twist his nose.'

He heard Joshua move. Then there was a sudden light and a

burst of sound. Charlie Rabbit twitched and his eyes shone with a deep, bright green glow; his paws went up and down, and his internal speaker began to hum.

Abbas pushed Charlie Rabbit into the gap above, then used the broken timber to shove the toy through, into the open air. As it emerged, the rabbit started to sing its trademark song:

Hoppity, hoppity, hoppity me, I'm as happy as I can be.
Carrot, lettuce, radishes, too, I'm Charlie Rabbit, how do you do?
Hoppity, hoppity, hoppity through, let's all be happy, too—

The song suddenly stopped.

Abbas waited, holding his breath, hoping that he would hear the stupid song start again, or someone call out to them, or something. But there was nothing. The chill water was up under his arms, rising even more swiftly now.

'Joshua,' said Abbas quietly. 'Crawl up as far as you can and put your face against that hole. Pull your legs up, out of the water.'

'Charlie Rabbit will get help,' said Joshua confidently, as he curled into a small ball.

'Yes,' said Abbas, in the darkness. He closed his eyes and let his head rest on the ground, close to the water that was caressing his neck. He was so cold now he couldn't really care what happened. 'Charlie Rabbit will get help.'

'Hoppity, hoppity, hoppity through, let's all be happy, too,' sang Joshua. 'Hoppity, hoppity... Abbas!'

'What?'

'Look, Abbas! Light!'

Abbas opened his eyes. The concrete block was rising up, rising into the air. Harsh, white electric light spilled down the chute, so bright he had to shield his eyes. Hands came reaching down to take Joshua, and then Abbas was lifted out himself, water spilling out on to the street behind him. Loud voices were all around him, shouting, asking questions, too much noise for Abbas to make any sense of it, save for one small voice that cut through everything. Joshua's voice, shrill in the night.

'Charlie! I want my Charlie Rabbit!'

BRIAN JACQUES

sergeant mugworth and algy buttons

ILLUSTRATIONS BY PAUL HESS

Since the world was young one day,
folks have oft been heard to say.
'Snakes are evil, snakes are bad,
they're a fear we've always had.'
Eyes that catch and hold you tight,
fangs which find you in the night,
sliding rustling coiling scales,
fearsome heads and swishing tails,
squirting poison, dealing death,
stilling heart and stopping breath,
wand'ring through your dreams you find,
serpents twisting through your mind,
cold, relentless, vicious, calm,
monster without leg or arm.
Who will save us, who indeed?
A champion is what we need,
a fighter for the common cause,
with knitted nose and stubby paws,
guardian of the infant cot,
brave, courageous, like as not,
whose rounded form and cuddly fur,
scorn reptile teeth and icy stare,
companion of the family's young,
your praises countless folk have sung,
belov'd of children everywhere.
Behold the simple Teddy Bear!

A devilsnake lay along the leafless wintered branches of the sycamore tree; it watched as the men below searched the gardens of Teasdale Avenue. There were police, qualified helpers from the Institute of Tropical Medicines and a snake expert, a herpetologist. High above, the devilsnake listened to their conversation drift up.

'Go carefully now, watch where you put your feet, it can lie on the ground like a piece of wood, completely still.'

'But you said it needs warmth, Mr Canovan, surely it can't survive for long in this winter without heat?'

'Hmm, that's the popular opinion in South America where the devilsnake lives. But there have been recorded cases of these reptiles living for quite a while in low temperatures, providing they can find some occasional warmth and a ready food supply.'

'Well personally I think it's pointless searching all these lofts, houses, basements, central-heating ducts and gardens. It could have perished from the cold or moved to another area completely.'

'No, it's my guess that the devilsnake is still around here somewhere, trying to establish a territory of its own. Three dead birds, a pet rabbit and two rats – at least it might not bother with people while it has plentiful supplies. Normally it wouldn't bother with fully-grown adult humans, but they have been known to try for small children. The man it bit was just unlucky to get in its way, though he's strong and with intensive care he'll probably pull through, thanks to modern serums.'

'But suppose it did bite a child or someone elderly. I think that the whole avenue should be moved out, all the residents, to a hotel or somewhere, until the thing is caught or killed.'

'Keep your voice down, we don't want a widespread panic in the neighbourhood over one snake. Maybe if it comes to a pinch the chief constable will give the word to evacuate this avenue.'

Luckily there were no residents about to hear the conversation. Only the devilsnake in the overhead branches and the two teddy bears. They sat next to each other in Alice Figgins' bedroom on the window ledge overlooking the back garden. The older teddy, Sergeant Mugworth, nodded slightly towards the devilsnake. 'Gurr!* You'd think they'd at least look up, we always did when I was out in India with Miss Alice's grandma.'

The smaller and newer of the two bears, a stout home-made little bruin with trouser-button eyes, gazed unblinkingly at the reptile. 'Bruhh!* The devilsnake can see us, it knows we're here, Sarge.'

'Gahrumm!* So it should, young Algy Buttons, m'bear, so it should. Now if this were India we'd have a mongoose to guard the house and family. But being back in Blighty as we are, it is our solemn duty to protect home and hearth. Remember what I've always said.'

'Brumff!* You mean that the sawdust we are stuffed with is Heart of Oak and old England for ever, Sarge?'

* Gurr - Small expression of disgust. Abbreviation of 'Gurrcha'
* Bruhh - I think * Gahrumm - Who cares? * Brumff - Certainly

'Guurd!* And don't you forget it my bruin, as of now we are the Figgins household mongooses.'

'Burrp!* Don't you mean mongeese, Sarge?'

'Nurrh!* Mongooses is the plural, no such thing as mongeese. You're a mongoose, young Algy, take my growl for it.'

'Hroom!*' said Algy Buttons. 'I don't feel much like a mongoose.'

'Grunn!* You've a lot to learn, young Algy, bear up now and keep your buttons peeled on that serpent out there.'

* * *

The day wore on without success for the searchers as they combed the gardens, shook the hedges and even used a flexible mechanised rod to probe the drains. Darkness fell, and they abandoned the hunt for that day. A police inspector and several constables went from house to house, warning and reassuring the occupants.

'No cause for alarm, sir, the creature's most likely dead from exposure in this weather. Please close all doors and lock all windows though, and if I were you I'd block any gaps at the bottoms of doors, no sense not taking precautions. If you should see anything suspicious, don't attempt to approach it, snake or no snake. Phone the number on this card and we'll be round immediately. Good night sir, we'll be back at eight tomorrow morning.'

* Gurrd - Good * Burrp - Excuse me * Nurrh - Nonsense * Hroom - Hohum * Grunn - Tch tch

The devilsnake watched until the gardens were free of human presence before it slithered out of the tree. Like a dark, silent, well-oiled machine it slid through the grass, contracting and expanding its sinuous body.

Now that night had come, the bears came to life properly. Sergeant Mugworth stood up, pressing his muzzle against the windowpane he watched the snake gliding across the lawn. It stopped when he rapped the glass with his paw.

'Gurrwooh!* Go on, clear off you great worm!'

The devilsnake heard, it turned and reared high, staring towards the bedroom window, its tongue flickering evilly as it hissed.

'Ssssss! I go now to feed, later I will come back and enter this house. I have plenty of death juice in my fangs, enough to kill you all, wait and see.'

Young Algy dropped on all fours roaring fiercely.

'Groowrr!* Just you try it, you don't frighten us, we're mongeese, er, I mean mongooses.'

Mugworth placed a restraining paw on his young assistant.

'Guffwuff!* Leave this to me, I've dealt with vermin like this in India, long before you were thought of, bruin. You need to be firm with snakes, show 'em who's boss, like this.'

Before the sergeant could remonstrate further the devilsnake had wriggled off through the hedge to the Ransome household

* Gurrwooh - Hey you * Groowrr - Come on * Guffwuff - Stand aside

next door. Algy Buttons performed a triumphant pawstand on the window ledge.

'Groohee!* We showed that oversized bootlace a thing or two, Sarge, no wonder he beat it pretty quick.'

Sergeant Mugworth wiped his brow on the curtain.

'Guff!* That's an old trick, Algy, he'll be back tonight, so stop that balancing upside down and stand up straight. We've an entire family to protect here. There's Nanna and Grandad, Miss Alice, her mummy and daddy, and new baby James. When they're all in bed I'll patrol the house. You must stay here and protect Miss Alice. Keep a lookout at this window – "*softly, softly, catchee monkey*", as we used to say out in India.'

'Whuh?* I thought we were after snakes not monkeys.'

'Hushmm!* Here comes Miss Alice, be still until she's asleep.'

* * *

Wintry clouds scurried across a moonless sky, chased by low moaning winds; it was no fit night for man or teddy to be abroad. In all the gardens of Teasdale Avenue only one living thing moved, the devilsnake. Caressing the rough brickwork and sliding leisurely over smooth paintwork it glided forward, hissing contemptuously. Humans were no match for a silent hunting snake, they were soft, fleshy, frightened and slow. They lived in their warm houses, stupidly thinking that a spell of chilly weather

* Groohee - Whoopee * Guff - Huh! * Whuh - What? * Hushmm - Silence

would kill off a fully-grown devilsnake. They knew nothing about the wasted, scorched earth of the South American rainforest created by their kind. The snake did, it had been forced to leave the charred forest for the foothills of the sierras, where the nights were cold, damp and hostile. It had survived capture by Indians and confinement in an old cane basket. Hardship? The devilsnake knew all about that. Travelling for weeks without food in an old leaky canoe, unable to get a bite at its fellow passengers in misery: monkeys, parakeets and other small creatures being shipped to the coast. The devilsnake was almost dead when it was gripped tightly by the neck in steel forceps. It dangled, wriggling feebly as the buyer held it up for inspection.

'Yep, this one'll do if it lives. Devilsnake, oh, an endangered species – not often you get a prime fully-grown adult like this.'

The devilsnake spent several more weeks being buffeted about on the ocean crossing. Hidden in a virtually airless metal container, it survived bad food, wet, rusty surroundings and the constant vice of the metal forceps, checking to see if it was still alive.

Hissing malevolently, it unwound itself from a drainpipe and slipped through a half-open transom window. Survival, in this soft new country, had been easy from the first illegal pet shop the dealer had sold it to. Escape had been simple, it had merely to bide its time, lying quite still as if dead. The moment came when a careless man left the top of the container only slightly open and turned away, a white mouse dangling from his gloved hand.

'Hey Jeff, come and take a look at this South American snake. I think they've sold us a dead 'un.'

Jeff arrived just in time to see the sinister reptile uncoil swiftly from the container on to the backroom floor, very much alive.

'Jackie, you dummy, you've let it escape. Here, chuck me that glove and get out of the way.'

The rear exit, facing a grassy field, was wide open. Jeff pulled the glove on, circling to block the doorway. He crouched to face the snake, reaching cautiously out with the heavy-leather-gloved hand. Unfortunately he was no match for the speed and ferocity of a wild devilsnake. Wriggling under his hand it struck, burying sharp, venomous fangs deep into his bare arm, slightly below the bicep.

'Yeeaargh! Jackie, it's bitten me. Help!'

With breathtaking swiftness the snake was out through the open door and whipping across the field, leaving behind a man shivering and moaning upon the floor, while his companion stood by, ashen with shock and indecision. The devilsnake made its way straight into the protective shrubbery of Teasdale Avenue gardens, freedom and a new environment. When the ambulance arrived, Jeff made his way straight into intensive care, with the assistance of two ambulance staff.

* * *

The Ransome family were watching television, unaware that they had an uninvited guest. Like a black shadow moving past the living-room door, the devilsnake slipped silently across the hallway. In the breakfast room Gary Ransome's gerbil pattered its tiny paws, drumming against the bottom of its cage in a futile attempt to raise the alarm. The reptile oozed its way around the open door, attracted by the noise. Weaving across the carpet the devilsnake focused its eyes, twin red-flecked orbs of emerald green. Now the gerbil had stopped drumming, but the hunter's keen senses detected the fluttering of panicked breath.

'Sssstill, be sssstill!'

There was a moment's pause, then the gerbil died of fright, its tiny heart stopped by the vision of evil. Furiously the devilsnake battered and butted at the woven-wire cage with its blunt head, but to no avail. The victim's body bounced and jolted about, secure inside its metal prison. The snake curled its coils around the cage, crushing it out of recognition; it bit at the wire, vainly trying to get at the delicious morsel inside. Finally, thwarted of its prey, it slid swiftly down the hallway. Mrs Ransome had the front door open, she was bending to put the empty milk bottles on the step as the devilsnake brushed by her leg on its way out. She stared at the dark rustling length vanishing into the shrubbery, then let out a high-pitched scream.

'Harreeeeee! Oohooh! Omylordmydearmygoodnessyurrk-urrghwaaaah!'

Harry Ransome came waddling out in his slippers. 'What is it Doris?' He hugged his overweight wife who was shaking like a jelly.

'Whoohoo! Harry, it was the snevildake!'

'Snevildake, what's a snevildake, dear?'

'Oh let go of me and phone the police you fool. I know a snevildake when I see one.'

*   *   *

Alice Figgins took both her teddy bears to bed, they lay either side of her, patiently waiting until the little girl fell asleep. After half an hour or so, Algy Buttons gently freed himself from her arm and slid down the duvet cover to the floor.

'Whukkup!* Come on, Sarge, time for nightbearwatch. Tut tut, don't tell me you've gone to bo-bo's.'

'Ammuwukk!* Er, what bo's? Never heard anything so ridiculous, young bruin. I used to lie awake with both eyes shut out in India, it's an old army trick. Here, lend a paw, Algy.'

The youngster assisted his sergeant from the bed. Mugworth attempted a few deep-fur bends and teddling on the spot to show he was wide awake and ready for anything.

'Whoff!* That's better, right, you hold the fort here. I'm off downstairs to patrol the premises.'

Algy clambered up the curtains on to the windowsill. Turning, he saluted to Sergeant Mugworth who was padding the door ajar.

* Whukkup - Wake up!   * Ammuwukk - I'm awake   * Whoff - Phew

'Wuwh!* What'll you do if you find the snake, Sarge?'

'Huggu!* I'll show him what trouble "bruin" really means. You take good care of Miss Alice now, Algy.'

Algy Buttons marched up and down the windowsill, performing smart about-turns, but secretly longing to be back snug in bed.

There were no live pets in the Figgins household, though there had been in previous years. A long-forgotten catflap in the rear door provided a simple entrance for the devilsnake. Its keen senses alert, the reptile curled itself around a coat stand in the hall, draped for all the world like a rolled silk scarf. It watched Mugworth laboriously descending the stairs, step by step. The snake appraised the old teddy bear, strange… it had the same scent pattern as a small human – that and an indefinable tang like aged velvet and powdered wood. As the sergeant reached ground level the devilsnake unfolded itself from the coats and dropped to the carpet. It reared up, facing Mugworth, hissing dangerously as it fixed its killing stare on him. The old sergeant was not about to show fear.

'Hrruw!* It's no use trying to put a spell on me by staring like that, I fear nothing. Now be off with you, you silly cricket belt.'

The devilsnake did not waste breath arguing, it struck!

The teddy was bowled over by the force of the attack, still he

* Wuwh - I say .* Huggu - Oho! * Hrruw - Ha ha

managed to get all four paws around his enemy. Folding sinuously back on itself, the devilsnake struck again and again at the unprotected fur. Mugworth clung grimly on like a rodeo rider aboard a bucking bronco.

'Guhho!* Bite away, you villain, that sort of thing doesn't affect an ex-Indian sergeant.'

But it did. Despite the fact that the venom was wasted upon a teddy, Mugworth soon began to weaken from the sawdust leaking out of the fang punctures. The devilsnake shrugged him off and began coiling around his furry body to crush him.

Blaah blaah! Blaah blaah! Blaah blaah! Blaah blaah!

Flashing blue light illuminated the hallway, feet pounded outside. Mr Ransome's phone call to the police was being answered.

Releasing its victim, the snake sought hiding; as the Figgins family roused themselves it slid up the arm of an overcoat on the stand.

The snake lay well concealed as lights were switched on and people clattered about the house.

'Here Edna, I'll take the baby, give me the carrycot.'

'Grandad, what's happening? Where's Nanna?'

'She'll be down in a tick, Alice love, as soon as she's put her teeth in. Come on, let's get our coats on, we're being taken to the Royal Cumberland Hotel for the night.'

* Guhho - Go on

108

'The Royal Cumberland! Oh Dad, you're not putting that raggedy old tweed overcoat on. What would the neighbours think, seeing you going into a posh hotel dressed like a jumble sale. Here, put your new coat on, the one Phil and I bought you for Christmas.'

Grandad Figgins was about to put his arm into the coat that contained the devilsnake up its sleeve. Grumbling, he allowed his daughter to hang it back on the stand and help him into the new camel overcoat. 'Spend half me life being dressed by women.'

Nanna Figgins came downstairs and began remonstrating with the young fresh-faced policeman who was shepherding the family out into a waiting minibus.

'It's not snakes I'm worried about, young man, we had enough of them out in the Punjab. What about our house, it could be burgled while we're away for the night.'

The policeman helped her up the minibus step.

'Now don't you worry, Mrs Figgins, the premises will be well secured until we get round to searching them. Have a pleasant stay at the Cumberland. Posh, eh?'

Mrs Ransome was awaiting her neighbours inside the vehicle.

'Oh Edna, you should've seen the thing, it must have been twelve feet long with teeth like I don't know what. Ugh! It had one of those dreadful little tongues that slide in and out, and flicker a lot. I thought my time had come I don't mind telling you. I'll never forget it as long as I live, will I Harry?'

The exaggerations on the size of the snake and its teeth continued getting bigger each time Doris Ransome recounted her ordeal. The police minibus drove off down Teasdale Avenue.

Once more the house was dark and silent. Algy had witnessed the evacuation from his post at the bedroom window. Alice had searched the folds of her duvet for the two teddies until Grandad hurried her from the room. Algy Buttons sat on the ledge, wondering what to do next. He was only a very young Teddy, and as such was unsure of what to do without the sergeant, who had always been there to guide him. Now he was all alone with the lights out. The thought of his companion downstairs gave Algy fresh courage; drawing himself bearfully up he climbed down the curtains and made his way out on to the landing at the head of the stairs.

'Gurroh!* Are you down there, Sarge, it's me, Algy the mongoose.'

'Dhuworr!* I'm at the bottom of the stairs by the meter cupboard.'

'Hudda!* Be with you in a tick, Sarge.'

'Burrwherr!* Devilsnake's somewhere about, watch yourself, young cub.'

Algy checked himself on the third stair down at this news, for a moment he felt a surge of fear. He sat down, his trouser-button eyes searching the darkened hall below.

'Guthhn!* Are you all right, Sarge?'

'Nonurhh!* The slimy thing bit me and crushed me quite a bit.'

Indignation rushed to the tip of Algy's knitted nose. He scrambled down the remaining stairs roaring aloud, his bear spirit aroused.

'Growwrbroarr!* Look out, devilsnake, I'm Algy Buttons the Terrible Teddy of Teasdale Avenue!'

Mugworth sat with his back to the meter cupboard, gazing at a limp leg, his paws covering the bigger holes to stop the sawdust leaking out. Algy sat beside him and inspected the wounds. The sergeant was bearing himself bravely.

* Gurroh - Hello * Dhuworr - Down here * Hudda - Hold that * Burrwherr - Beware
* Guthhn - Nothing * Nonurhh - Not quite * Growwrbroarr - Teddy war cry

'Gumgum!* Not afraid of the sight of a little sawdust are you, cub?'

Algy stood up, averting his eyes from the stuffing.

'Graff!* You just lie still, I'll be back in a tick.'

Mugworth sat silent in the darkness, he was not sure where the snake had got to. Good as his growl, Algy returned promptly.

'Grubb!* Plum jam and Plasticine, this should do the trick, Sarge.'

He set to work patching the older bear up, Mugworth bore it all without complaint. When the surgery was completed he stood up like a true teddy, a little wobbly from lack of sawdust, but brave as a lion.

'Phwurr!* Don't know what that beast has in its teeth, but it makes a bruin feel quite woozy.'

Algy was not listening, he was watching the long dark shape as it unwound from the sleeve of an old tweed overcoat.

Further up Teasdale Avenue the search continued. Extra police had been drafted in, they were directed by Mr Canovan, the herpetologist. Gauntlets had been issued, plus forked sticks and heavy sacks; a medical team was standing by with a supply of serum. Constables Fitzpatrick and Hart suffered an unpleasant incident with a child's skipping rope. The herpetologist poked gingerly at a pair of black school tights on a bedroom floor.

* Gumgum - Come come * Graff - Who me? * Grubb - Righto * Phwurr - I'm sick

'I don't like this one little bit, couldn't it have waited until daylight? I'm half-asleep from searching all day.'

After a nasty moment when he became entangled with an oily towrope in a darkened garage, Inspector Mulhearn took to slashing about in dark corners with a gardening spade, damaging property left, right and centre.

'I'll chop the filthy thing in two if I get half a chance and ask questions later. Are we nearly finished in here now?'

Algy Buttons stood with his body shielding Sergeant Mugworth, the devilsnake swayed in front of him hissing.

'Ssssst, told you I'd be back, didn't I.'

The older bear pawed plum jam from his muzzle.

'Whukku!* Fat lot of good it's done you, the humans have all gone, so you can't get them, can you?'

'Sssst, maybe not right now, but I can always await their return. Meanwhile, I've cornered you and your little friend here.'

Algy played for time, his button eyes searching frantically around as he growled in his most menacing tones.

'Gorrawhurra!* You can't hurt us, we're mongeese, none of your nasty poison worked on my sergeant, did it.'

As he talked, he spotted the very thing he needed, a small gardening cane used for tying plants to, some knotted string was still fixed to the end of it. Mr Figgins had left it under the stairs last

* Whukku - Oh dear! * Gorrawhurra - So what?

Saturday afternoon when he was pottering about in the garden. Young Algy did not hesitate, he made a rush for it. The devilsnake struck, but he dodged to one side. Unfortunately he tripped on the serpent's coils; it wound itself tight around his leg. Struggling forward against the tugging coils, the little teddy stretched his paw towards the cane. The snake heaved him backwards, opening its jaws wide as it turned to sink hungry fangs into its victim. Mugworth acted courageously to save his friend, hurling himself upon the devilsnake he stuffed his head into its gaping mouth.

'Bruhhry!* Move yourself young 'un, it smells awful in here!'

Algy felt the coils relax as it tried to disgorge Mugworth's head. Stumbling free of the serpentine bonds, he grabbed the stout garden cane with both paws and attacked. The devilsnake was taken aback by the ferocity of the onslaught. Algy beat at its head with the stick, whipping it with the string and poking at the angry eyes, he belaboured away at the sensitive nostrils of the snake. The sergeant strove to free his muzzle from the needle-like fangs, kicking and punching as best as he could with all four paws. Over and over the three rolled and thrashed in the darkened hallway, both teddies striving heroically against the superior force of the maddened devilsnake. Finally, the snake managed to anchor its tail round the leg of the telephone table and fought free of its fierce assailants. Mugworth fell back,

* Bruhhry - Hurry

panting heavily. Algy knelt by his side, keeping a careful button eye on their foe.

'Brubbh!* Well, we certainly gave him what for, are you all right?'

'Ruggah!* Oh I'll pass muster, young cub. Look at that rascal, I think he's had enough – not hissing and waving his tail about so much now, is he. I'm tired, I suppose we'd better let him beat a retreat out of here. I don't think he'll bother us or our house again. What d'you say, young Algy?'

Outside the clouds had cleared, it was calmer too, the wind had dropped. Algy sat beside the sergeant, through the fanlight window over the front door he could see the sky. Two stars stood out like white gems.

'Burrzoh!* Look, Sarge, it's our spirits, Great Bear and Lesser Bear. They're watching over us: we must be true to them.'

Both Mugworth and the devilsnake looked on in amazement at young Algy Buttons. Taking up his gardening cane he cracked the string like a whip as he advanced upon the serpent.

'Groowrr!* Fight you miserable shoestring!'

The devilsnake could not focus on Algy's button eyes with their eight sewing holes. It bared its teeth menacingly at him.

'Ssst, let me be, foolish one, I will leave here and never return.'

Algy poked at its mouth with the stick.

'Bruhohoh!* I could not let children anywhere live in your evil

* Brubbh - Whew!   * Ruggah - Pretty fair   * Burrzoh - Up there   * Groowrr - Come on
* Bruhohoh - Not likely

shadow, I would be failing in my duty as a Teddy Bear. Come on, fight!'

'Bruhvoh!* That's the stuff, young Algy, we'll sort the blighter out between us. Help me up.'

Algy risked a backward glance.

'Grunho!* You've done enough, Sarge, stay close and do as I say. I'm in command for the present, you're not fit for fighting.'

Algy launched a headlong attack upon the snake, poking, clubbing, whipping and beating with all his might. The devilsnake released its hold on the table leg, striking and lashing it came at him.

'Sssst, I will destroy you, I will bite and rip, I will crush and squeeze until you are nothing but rags.'

Algy backed off along the hallway, still fighting back as the snake came after him like a dark avenging streak. Mugworth followed in their wake, the swishing tail knocked him flat several times. Algy was retreating according to his own plan, moving towards the kitchen, he kept up his beating and poking, making the devilsnake come forward after him. Only once did he shift his glance, to make sure the way was clear and unhindered: it was nearly the young bear's undoing.

The snake locked its jaws around the stick and began dragging him backwards. Algy dug his paws in the carpet, rucking up under them, as he pulled back with might and main.

* Bruhvoh - Bravo * Grunho - No, no

The sergeant bounced up and down on the lashing tail as Algy shouted.

'Suhhr!* Keep him coming forward, he must follow me!'

Mugworth did all he could at the tail end. Up at the head, Algy realised that the devilsnake could not strike with its jaws locked on the stick. He threw himself at its blunt nose, blocking the two sensitive airways with his body, he held on tight. The snake made angry muffled hisses as it shook itself to rid its head of the small smothering bear. Automatically, it was thrusting forward again. It managed to shake Algy off and started after him, furious and breathless at the teddy, as he ducked and dodged, thwacking away at the head of his enemy.

They entered the kitchen still fighting, sliding and slipping across the smooth vinyl-covered floor. Round the plastic wastebin they battled, Algy's short fur pierced in a dozen places by the relentlessly questing fangs, though he lost very little sawdust being young and firmly packed. The devilsnake's head was scraped and raked by the cane, its tongue swollen from where the small bruin had jumped upon it several times, scales were missing from its throat and one of its eyes was shutting from a nasty jab.

On they struggled, across a fallen ironing board, over a wet mop, through the legs of a tall stool, battling remorselessly. Sergeant Mugworth in the rear growled and roared encouragement.

* Suhhr - That's it!

'Gurrtedd!* Give him stick, lots of it, bash the bounder!'

Narrowly avoiding the slashing fangs, Algy called out, 'Bruhkk!* Open the white cupboard in the corner, Sarge. Hurry!'

'Wuchumm!* This one or this one, oh no, this one is only drawers.'

'Bruhkk!* The white cupboard in the corner. The white one!'

'Guhlug!* It's got a light inside!'

The shaft of light shining across the floor guided Algy as he retreated further, making his way towards it. Suddenly he turned and ran. The devilsnake, sensing victory, streaked forward after him.

With a clatter Algy leaped inside the white cupboard. Pushing aside hard bricks of butter and stiff vegetables he scrambled his way to the back of the white cupboard where he sat next to a circular dial.

The devilsnake slid into the white cupboard after Algy with a loud hiss of satisfaction.

'Ssssttt! Got you now, there's no way out, little one.'

Algy seized a silver-wrapped wedge of Danish blue cheese, which was way over the sell-by date and held it in front of him as a shield.

'Broww!* Shut the door, Sarge, slam it and jam it tight!'

'Ruggoh!* You'll be trapped, bruin, that's not the way we dealt with snakes out in India.'

'Buffah!* Never mind India, do as I say. Slam that door, now!'

* Gurrtedd - Go ted * Bruhkk - Quick * Wuchumm - Which one?
* Guhlug - Goodness me * Broww - Now! * Ruggoh - Silly! * Buffah - Silly yourself!

As the devilsnake struck, Algy held up his shield, angry fangs tore at the silver foil wrapping. Then the door slammed shut and the white cupboard was thrown into inky blackness. Algy relaxed back and gave a sigh of relief. 'Grooh!* Always wondered if that light went off when the door closed. Now I know.' Distracted by the curious light, the little bear didn't notice his back pressing against the circular dial, nor the sudden dip in temperature.

The snake slid about, trying to detect Algy among the different odours, but confident that it had him trapped.

'Sssst, can't get out now, can you little bear?'

Algy pushed a juice carton over, he heard the snake spit as it connected with a satisfying bump.

'Brugguk!* Neither can you, flathead!'

Mugworth wedged his back up against the white cupboard door, his feet planted firmly on the floor. He gazed up through the kitchen window. Even though the two stars were not visible, he talked to them.

'Brouu!* Keep him safe, he's only a little teddy bear doing his duty.'

At seven a.m. the next morning, sunlight flooded through the kitchen windows, making dark night and poisonous snakes seem a million years away. Inspector Mulhearn shifted the old teddy bear out of the way with his shoe as he opened the refrigerator to find milk for the tea that was brewing.

* Grooh - Hmmm!   * Brugguk - Take that!   * Brouu - Oh stars!

'Mr Canovan, over here. Look!'

The inspector's shout drew not only the herpetologist, but all the searchers in the house. They grouped round the fridge, shaking their heads at the sight of the frozen devilsnake. Mr Canovan picked up a short gardening cane from the floor and rooted the reptile out. It rattled upon the polished vinyl floor like a cracked dinnerplate. Ice between the coils had packed it into a neat circular mass, at the centre of which the rigid head stuck up, fangs protruding and eyes glazed over in a lifeless stare.

'Dead as a doornail, though why it made its way into a fridge is a complete mystery to me.'

Inspector Mulhearn swung the fridge door back and forth, he tested the hinges and rocked the cabinet vigorously. With an air of slightly superior smugness he lit a briar pipe, puffing reflectively and shaking the dead match as he propounded his theory.

'Quite simple really, this is an old fridge – as you can see the door practically swings open and shut on its own. Add to that the fact that the whole thing is balanced on an uneven floor – see how easily it rocks. Now, the snake would have seen the door partly open and pushed its way into the cabinet, causing the whole thing to wobble and allowing the door to swing slowly shut. Thus!'

He demonstrated by rocking the fridge until the door closed. Everyone nodded in agreement as the inspector opened the door and indicated the large bottom-shelf area.

'As I say, that's what happened. It's an old fridge, you see – personally I'd advise them to invest in a newer model, as this one's so faulty it freezes everything solid! – though luckily for us they didn't. Hmm, what's this at the back of the dairy and juice department. A frozen teddy bear. The child must have been playing some sort of game. Sit him in the sink where the sunlight'll thaw him out, Constable Hart.'

'Right sir, I'll put this other fellow in there to keep him company. He looks a bit knocked about, covered in jam and modelling clay – that's kids for you. Perhaps it was the two teddy bears who tricked the snake into the fridge, sir.'

The inspector squinted an eye at Hart through a fragrant cloud of pipe tobacco. 'How old are you, Constable Hart?'

'Twenty-three, sir.'

'Then start acting your age, sonny. Get this snake ready for Mr Canovan to take back to his laboratory. No doubt you'd like to take it back to the university for tests, eh?'

The herpetologist watched as Hart gingerly slid the frozen devilsnake into a supermarket carrier bag.

'Thank you inspector, actually I don't think I'll be dissecting this fellow. I'll get him straight into deep-freeze: he'll make an interesting talking point with my zoology graduates.'

A full moon shone on the windowledge that night. Sergeant Mugworth and Algy Buttons sat gazing at the sky, completely relaxed. Both bears had been restuffed, resewn, washed and dried out; Alice's nanna had made them as good as new again.

'Spruhh!* I feel like a young cub again, bruin.'

'Wulluh!* You look very smart, Sarge. It's nice to feel all clean and fluffy again, though I wasn't too keen on that bath.'

'Gruttu!* Just one thing, young Algy. How did you ever survive the whole night in that white cupboard? You were stiff as a board when they rescued you, completely frozen white.'

'Gurgohh!* It was a plan of my own, sorry I disobeyed your orders, Sarge. I got fed up of being a mongeese and pretended I was a polar bear; they don't mind the cold, you see.'

'Brugglaihgrooh!'*

The two teddy bears watched their twin stars twinkling in the night sky, far away and high above the restored tranquillity of Teasdale Avenue.

* Spruhh - Look at me * Wulluh - Indeed * Gruttu - Truthfully now * Gurgohh - Simple really
* Brugglaihgrooh - It's mongoose, not mongeese

BRIAN PATTEN

miss shush

ILLUSTRATION BY NATHAN REED

Miss Shush was always going
'*Shush*!'
'*Shush*!' said Miss Shush.
You couldn't do anything without Miss Shush going, '*Shush*!'
If you simply breathed loudly, she'd go, '*Shush*!'
And you'd have to hold your breath till you gasped
And if you gasped too loudly
She'd make you stay behind after school.
Miss Shush was a pain in the—
'*Shush*!'
When a gigantic hungry tiger
With big yellow fangs and huge sharp claws
And an insatiable appetite for teachers
Escaped from the zoo
And sneaked up behind Miss Shush
Guess what we said to each other?
'*Shush*!'

MARIANNE CURLEY
the star

There's a new girl at school today. I spot her the second she walks through the front gates. She's alone and seems to be headed in my direction. I take another look. The girl has pale skin and dark hair to her shoulders. She sees me and for a second our eyes collide. Hers are amazing – so light, they could pass as grey, with just the slightest hint of green. They remind me of a fox. I can't look away.

She comes right up to where I'm sitting on a bench. 'You're a psychic, aren't you?'

Her words are so direct they stun me. I get defensive quickly. 'Maybe. Who wants to know?'

'My name's Erin. But I don't have time for small talk. I need your services.'

I can't believe her abruptness. Most people wouldn't dream of mentioning my paranormal ability. In fact, they tend to stay well away, just in case I perform some sort of hocus-pocus on them. That's why I sit alone most of the time. They're scared. But not this girl. 'My *services* are not for sale.'

'I don't have money anyway. I just need your help.'

For some reason I find myself intrigued. It could be her strange eyes. I'm not sure. It could be the sadness I see inside them.

Deep inside. 'Tell me why I should help you?'

'Because there's nobody else.'

'What do you want me to do?'

'Find my brother. He's the only one left that's still missing.'

This is getting weird. 'What are you talking about?'

'My brother is lost in the forest that spreads west of Glenhaven.'

'Glenhaven? Isn't that...?'

'Over the border, but there's a train that will get us there in four hours.'

I vaguely recall hearing something on the news this past week. Not that I listen to the news very often lately. Since my psychic power grew stronger, my mind never seems to rest any more. But I do remember hearing about a family that went hiking at Glenhaven. There was a flash flood and the three children became separated from their parents. One of the children was found on the first day. But apparently one is still missing. 'How old is he?'

She frowns. 'Only six. He doesn't know how to fend for himself. He doesn't know how to find food or water. He won't last another night.'

'How do you know this?'

'I know my brother!' she yells. 'And you have the power to find him!'

Her anger makes me suspicious. I get up quickly. My backpack, and everything inside, spills out. 'Is this a joke? Who sent you? It's not funny, you know. Do you think I like being like this? Ignored as if I'm invisible, or being made fun of?'

'I wasn't making fun of you,' she says in a much softer tone, a tone bordering on pleading. 'I really need your help. My brother is in trouble.' She puts a hand to her throat, resting her open palm on her chest. 'I feel him, in here. I know he's still alive.'

I peer at her, trying to work out if she's for real. 'Just because he's the last one of you to be found, doesn't mean the rescue teams are going to give up looking for him. They found you, didn't they?'

For the first time she breaks eye contact. Her head rolls around the base of her throat as if she is completely worn out. Well, I guess she would be. She must have suffered quite an ordeal herself. And now she's here, hours away, trying to get me to help her. I glance into her eyes. From this close they look like silver. She trembles and turns an even paler shade of pale. I think she's going to pass out. Finally she says, 'They're looking in the wrong direction!'

'So why don't you tell them?'

'Do you think I haven't tried? They won't listen to me! They just think I'm some stupid little girl who doesn't know anything.' She quickly adds, 'Please, just say you'll do it. You've helped others. I know about you helping the police find that kidnapped little girl.'

Yeah, I remember too. It had drained me for days afterwards. The publicity surrounding the event catapulted my loner status.

'Will you help me, Luke?'

She knows my name even though it wasn't printed in the papers. The thought makes me laugh. Obviously, she knows a lot more about me than just my name! 'When is this train?'

'Huh?'

'The train that will take us to Glenhaven?'

'It leaves in fifteen minutes.'

I grab my bag and look about. No one is watching. 'We'd better hurry then.'

The train is already sitting at the station. I glance up and down the platform. A porter is loading luggage into the baggage compartment at one end. 'We don't have a ticket.'

'I told you I don't have any money.' She runs straight into a carriage.

Well, neither do I. I glance around and follow quickly. She gets me to hide in the toilet when the conductor makes an appearance. When he's gone we find seats in a half-empty carriage. Suddenly I wish I hadn't agreed to help her. What are the chances that her brother is still alive? He's only six and has been missing for seven days! An hour ago we hadn't even met. Yet strangely there's an unexplained rightness to her sitting beside me, a comfortable feeling, as if I've known her all my life.

I must have fallen asleep. I wake with a jolt and Erin shouting in my face, 'Come on, Luke! We're here!'

I grab my backpack and follow her out of the carriage and all the way to the end of the rapidly emptying platform. There, she jumps down on to the tracks.

'Hey, what are you doing?'

'Come on!'

A helicopter overhead flies in a northerly direction. I stare at it for a minute. That's where the rescue teams are searching, but Erin is adamant on going west. I jump down behind her. I haven't come all this way to back out now.

She crosses the track without even looking. More carefully, I follow. From there we hike down a path that leads us right into the base of the valley. We come to a creek with a bridge over the top. We cross it and find ourselves immersed in dense forest. I follow Erin off the path. We keep walking into thicker forest, and the time passes quickly. My stomach growls. 'Hey!' I call out. 'Wait a minute.'

She spins round.

'We've been walking for ages. Let me get an apple out of my lunch box.'

She groans and rolls her eyes. 'But it's going to get dark soon!' Her voice sounds panicked. She stares off into the thick forest surrounding us. Just as I find my apple I hear her say softly, 'Tyler is scared of the dark.'

I think she's going to cry. Not quite sure what to do, I thrust my hand out, offering her the apple. 'I don't know how you can think of food!' she snaps, taking off.

We keep going, wading through miles of thick forest growth, and with each step it becomes darker. Spiders start weaving webs between branches. A possum gives a squeal as it clambers up a tree to my right. I glance round with a sinking feeling kicking into my stomach, as I realise exactly where I am – in the middle of thick forest as night is starting to descend. 'Hey!'

She turns. 'What's wrong now?'

I cross my arms over my chest. 'OK. Firstly, I'm not in the habit of taking a compass to school, so I'm assuming you know the way out of here? And secondly, I didn't bring a torch. And well, you didn't bring *anything*. Not even water! Didn't you learn a thing from your recent experience?'

Tears spring to her eyes. Oh no! This is all I need. But there's one more point I want to bring up. 'My mother's got to be worried like hell by now.'

'I'm sorry,' she mumbles, glancing at her feet. 'I swear we're nearly there.' She looks up and stares straight into my eyes. 'Don't bail on me now, Luke.'

As if I could with those sad eyes looking at me! 'OK. But when I searched for that little girl I had her clothing in my hand. I even had a recently lost tooth that her mother had kept for the tooth fairy.'

From around her neck, Erin unhooks a chain. She holds it out to me and I open my hand to take it. On the end of the chain is a gold cross with a sparkling stone in its centre.

'It's mine,' she says. 'But, well, we're brother and sister, so that means we're linked, right?'

I nod, and she adds, 'When Tyler was little he used to reach up and play with it. He loved the glistening crystal. He called it a star.'

My fingers fold around the chain and cross and I consciously think of Tyler. In seconds my head fills with a sense of him. He's in pain and keeps drifting in and out of consciousness. He's also afraid. Very afraid. I open my eyes. Erin was right all along. He's in this area somewhere. 'He's not far.'

She smiles and her eyes practically glow.

'I'll find him now,' I reassure her.

I take the lead, firmly holding on to the cross and chain. Erin follows. We leap over a shallow creek, winding our way up a rising embankment. The ground rapidly becomes moist and we have to be careful not to slip. It takes ages, but finally I get an overwhelming sense that Tyler is very close. His fear is seeping through every nerve in my body. My head starts to throb and ache.

'What is it?' Erin calls out. 'Is something wrong with Tyler?'

I take the chain and cross and thread my hand through it, wrapping the chain twice around my wrist. The cross dangles into my palm. It's my link to Tyler and I don't want to lose it. I start searching again, positive the boy is nearby. I clasp my right palm over the cross and press my two hands together and think of Tyler. Sensations of his nearness fill my head, so strong I have to close my eyes and force myself to breathe slowly.

'Luke, what's wrong?'

I open my eyes and see him leaning up against the base of a large tree. His eyes are closed and his chest is hardly moving, but I know he's still alive.

I run over and the first thing that hits me is his size. He's so small, huddled up against the tree, one leg curled up, the other straight. It's then I notice the twisted angle of his bones. Straight away I throw my backpack down, digging inside for my ruler and anything else that could make a splint.

Erin squats beside me. Tears are pouring down her face, obviously tears of relief. She knows her brother is going to be safe. I can't help a quick look around. It's so dark now, how on earth are we going to find our way out of here?

'I'll show you the way,' Erin says softly.

I look up and she swallows deeply in her throat. 'Water,' she mumbles.

I dig my bottle out and offer it to her. She shakes her head. 'For him.'

I take the bottle to Tyler's mouth and trickle some water across his lips. He stirs and sips. 'Slowly,' I warn. His eyes flutter open briefly and he sips again, before drifting off into unconsciousness. I look across at Erin. 'He's going to be all right.'

She nods but appears unable to speak. I finish the makeshift splint and carefully lift the boy into my arms. A fragment of the moon breaks through the canopy above, enough to see the boy more clearly. He has scratches and bite marks all over his exposed skin. He's been through a nasty ordeal, but soon he'll be back with his parents. The whole family will be together again. I should be happy at the thought, but I can't shrug this eerie feeling of gloom. I put the sensations down to being tired and hungry.

'Are you ready, Luke?' Erin asks.

I nod and she starts to lead the way out. She seems to know where she's going and, well, I don't. So I follow, trusting her. She hasn't been wrong so far.

After a while my arms grow weary and numb. I make her stop three or four times to give them a rest and get rid of the pins and needles that keep plaguing me. After a couple of hours I move Tyler's body to my right shoulder. He's still out cold, but I can feel his little heart beating, while the skin of his face warms my neck.

The forest starts to thin out and I realise we're back in the valley. Light from a full moon makes the way much clearer. The bridge looms into sight, welcoming us like a doorway to paradise. On the other side lights come into focus and I hear noises unlike anything I've been listening to these last few hours in the forest. I soon realise the noises are human sounds. People, talking or bustling about.

The lights become stronger. I get a second wind at the sight of them. It must be the railway station. But as we draw nearer I start wondering why the station is so vividly lit. Spotlights are everywhere. Some lights are even moving through the bushes towards us.

Someone calls out and soon the sounds of thumping footsteps draw close. A man in bright yellow overalls runs over. 'Are you Luke Stanton?'

I nod, my mouth too dry to form words.

He takes Tyler from my arms carefully. 'You found the boy.'

Others quickly surround us. Some are in overalls like the first man, others are in white. Someone puts a drinking flask to my lips. I sip greedily. 'Take it easy,' says a man who hasn't shaved for a few days. 'How did you know...?' He shakes his head. 'Don't answer. I've heard about you. You scared your mother half to death when you didn't come home from school today.'

'How did she know I was here?'

'When she found out you hadn't turned up for any classes she went checking at your local bus stop and railway station. Someone recognised your photograph and told her they saw you boarding a train headed out this way. She guessed you might be here trying to help.' His head shakes again. 'She's over at the search-and-rescue base we've had set up for the Wilson family this past week. We'll let her know right away that you're OK.'

We get to the station and someone throws a blanket around my shoulders.

'What about the boy?' I ask.

The man with the blanket points to an ambulance with its back doors wide open. An ambulance officer comes over to check me out.

'The boy?' I ask her. 'Is he all right?'

'He's dehydrated, has a broken leg and some nasty infected scratches. We're getting some fluids into him now, then he's off to the hospital for further treatment. But I think he's going to be fine. It's a miracle he survived, that's for sure. It's as if someone has been looking after him.'

'Yeah, of course,' I say. 'If only you'd listened to her in the first place, you could have found Tyler sooner.'

The ambulance officer peers at me with narrowed eyes. 'What are you talking about?'

'His sister Erin.'

Around me everyone goes quiet and strangely still.

'When did you see Erin?'

I almost groan out loud. Are these people dense or something? 'She's right behind me.' I spin round to show them, but can't see Erin anywhere. The blanket falls from my shoulders as I walk around looking for her. A strange sense of unreality settles in my stomach. What's going on here?

'Erin?' I call out.

The man who hasn't shaved in three days puts his hands on my shoulders from behind. 'I think you'd better come with me, son.'

I shrug him off. 'No! I have to find Erin. She must have fallen away. I remember crossing the bridge together. The moon was out. I saw her clearly.'

The ambulance officer tries to put the blanket back over my shoulders, but I shrug it off. 'She's out there. You have to go and find her. She can't be far!'

The ambulance officer puts her hands on my face, one on either side. I have nowhere to look except straight into her eyes. 'Listen to me, Luke. We found Erin.'

Relief hits me and I smile.

Then she says, 'In the early hours of this morning. On the northern side of the railway bridge.'

I can't believe what this woman is trying to tell me.

She looks at me intensely. 'Luke, Erin had been dead for at least six hours before the rescue team found her.'

Moisture hits the back of my eyes as I try to take this in. My head shakes and I find I have to lunge for breath. I break out of the ambulance officer's hold, spinning away. Someone in the background mutters to the others to leave me alone. I'm grateful for the quiet moment to figure this out. It's a hard concept to follow, even for me! When Erin came to see me this morning she was already dead. She wasn't real. So what was she? Did I imagine her presence? Were my senses working on some strange level that I'm not even aware of?

My eyes catch sight of something shimmering near my hand. I look down and stare, unblinking. There, wrapped around my wrist, is Erin's gold cross and chain.

PHILIP ARDAGH

the cabinet of curiosities

ILLUSTRATION BY ROBIN JARVIS

In London, in a blind alley off one of the warren of small roads that
crisscross between Charing Cross Station and Oxford Street,
there is a shop called The Cabinet of Curiosities. According to the

faded gold lettering on a wooden sign to the right of the door, the proprietor's name was – or is – a Mr de Ville, and the shop was established in 1835. There certainly seem to have been few, if any, changes to the building since then. The brickwork is blackened with the grime of years: soot from the days when smoke poured from everyone's chimney and every train was powered by steam, fuelled by coal.

I come upon the shop quite by chance. With Christmas approaching, I've been up in town for a meeting with the bishop and, afterwards, to buy a box of 'Chocolate Olivers' from the food hall at Fortnum & Mason. Both tasks having been successfully completed, and it being such a beautiful winter's afternoon, I decide to do some window-shopping before heading off to catch my train home. Unfortunately, the beautiful afternoon soon turns into a very wet one and, having left the vicarage this morning without an umbrella, my first priority is to beg, steal or preferably buy one. (I jest, of course. Being a clergyman, begging or stealing is not on the agenda.)

I am about to dash down a side street to where I have a vague recollection of having previously seen a shop specialising in tobacco and walking sticks, suspecting that it'll be *just* the kind of place that will also sell umbrellas, when a traditional furled gent's black brolly catches my eye in the brightly lit window of this shop down an alley to my right. Splashing through recently formed puddles, I push open the door, triggering the most satisfying jangling of a bell above my head as I step inside.

I fall in love with The Cabinet of Curiosities in this instant. As a young child I was taken to see the pantomime *Aladdin* and, when the principal boy found the cave full of treasure – the rock face apparently sliding aside to the command of 'Open Sesame!' – there was a thin gauze curtain between the audience and the cave's contents, giving the 'treasure' beyond it a hazy, dreamlike and undefined quality. It was left to each member of the audience to imagine exactly what that treasure might be. As well as piles of gold coins and jewels and crowns, I had imagined other fantastical objects...

...And here are just such items, crammed from floor to ceiling of this tiny shop: a telescope; an astrolabe; life-size animals – some carved, some moulded, some simply stuffed; a ship's wheel; a throne-like chair apparently made entirely from seashells; leather-bound books; extraordinary paintings; masks; hats; crystal balls; clocks. My head spins at the possibilities of what I might find.

A small neatly dressed white-haired man comes out from behind a polished wooden counter, edged with strips of brass. 'Good afternoon, reverend,' he says. Scarf-less, my dog collar is clearly visible. Despite his obvious great age – his skin looks thin and dry – his eyes sparkle with youthful vitality and his voice is loud and strong. 'My name is Theo de Ville,' he says. 'Welcome to The Cabinet of Curiosities.'

'Good afternoon, sir,' I smile, and then, catching sight of what appears to be a piece of blood-stained woman's clothing hanging up behind him, ask him, with some surprise, what such a thing is doing here.

'It belonged to Alexandra, the last Empress of Russia,' says de Ville, gently fingering a sleeve. 'She was wearing this very garment when she and her family were murdered by the Bolsheviks in July 1918.'

'The Lord have mercy!' I gasp, but I have to admit (to myself at least) that it is strangely fascinating; this piece of history reduced to something so mundane. I step forward to take a closer look, knocking the edge of a small cane table, causing something to fall from it.

With remarkable speed for a man of any age, de Ville's hand shoots out and catches the precious item before any damage is done. This swift action brings to mind a frog shooting out its long sticky tongue at high speed, catching an unsuspecting bug in flight.

'I'm so sorry,' I say. 'That was very clumsy of me. What is that?'

'An old tankard,' says the shopkeeper, holding up the dull grey object, 'with no intrinsic value, but rich in historical association. The playwright Christopher Marlowe was drinking from this pewter mug moments before becoming embroiled in a knife fight that was to result in his murder. The date was sometime in May 1593, the place was Deptford.'

'Extraordinary!' I say, as a trickle of sweat runs from my temple down to my chin. The place has been getting noticeably warmer since I first came inside. 'Your shop is indeed a cabinet of curiosities! Does every item on sale here have such an incredible history?'

'Choose any object, reverend,' de Ville suggests.

I unbutton my heavy winter coat and pick my way through the vast array of stock, deciding to rise to the challenge by looking for the most uninteresting object I can find amongst this extraordinary cornucopia. I finally settle for what appears to be little more than a square of faded cloth inside a glass jar. I hold the jar up to the light to inspect its contents more closely. Let Theo de Ville make an interesting story out of *this*, I think. 'What about this?' I ask.

'You seem to be attracted to the morbid, Reverend Morris,' says de Ville, his old, old face breaking into a smile. 'This piece of cloth was the very flannel being used by Jean Paul Marat, a leader in the French Revolution, when he was stabbed to death in his bath in July 1793.'

I study the rag with mixed emotions. Either Mr de Ville is an excellent liar or I have stumbled upon one of the most extraordinary shops in the whole of London, if not England, the United Kingdom, Great Britain or the British Isles!

Then another thought occurs to me. 'How do you know my name, sir?' I ask.

'No great mystery there, reverend.' The shopkeeper smiles once more. 'With your coat now unbuttoned and your nametape sewn into the lining...'

Of course! Mrs Tompkin, the housekeeper I inherited along with the vicarage, insists on labelling all my coats, jackets, trousers, shirts and more. Not even my undergarments escape such treatment! I smile back, feeling a little disappointed that the truth isn't somehow more out of the ordinary and more in keeping with this curious place of curiosities. My disappointment obviously shows.

'Most tricks lose their magic once explained,' Mr de Ville comments. 'Are you in a particular hurry to be anywhere?'

I think of the rain outside and the fact that trains run every half-hour to my parish. 'I'm in no hurry at all,' I confess.

'Then would you like me to acquaint you with some of our more interesting items?' he suggests. 'It would be my pleasure to do so, reverend.'

And I agree, which is how I come to be spending a most fascinating December afternoon in The Cabinet of Curiosities, whilst the rain beats down outside.

Two thoughts keep recurring as Mr Theo de Ville delights in showing me his extraordinary treasures (all, apparently, for sale). First is the dawning realisation that there is, of course, the possibility that nothing he is telling me is true. This could be the sales patter of a consummate salesman inviting me to buy what is little more than worthless junk and second-hand goods. Is a single one of these objects surrounding me in The Cabinet of Curiosities what Mr de Ville actually purports it to be? How can I tell if an item really has been worn by the Empress Alexandra or used by Christopher Marlowe, for example? One apparently blood-stained garment or battered pewter mug, must, I would have thought, look very much like another. Are the contents of this shop as much a part of make-believe as the treasures in that pantomime Aladdin's cave? Anyone can label a pickled mouse in a jar 'A Companion to Sir Thomas More During His Confinement in The Tower of London Prior To His Execution In July 1535'. Is all of this a hoax? A conceit? An elaborate joke?

To be fair to the proprietor, who is now holding up an item which he says is the molten remains of a bracelet worn by Joan of Arc when she was burned at the stake in the marketplace in Rouen in May 1431, it's possible that these aren't the right questions to be asking. What matters is the magic. Those who choose to believe that the telescope they have in their hands was once used by Galileo Galilei gain as much pleasure from the act as if holding one proven to be so. I know much about faith – it is my calling, and my profession – and what this shop offers is the promise of some kind of connection with exciting events in history. I want this *promise* to be fulfilled. I'm willing it. I *want* what de Ville is telling me to be true.

The second thought to recur, as I am conducted on this guided tour of the merchandise, is just how much of it seems to be connected to death. I've yet to be shown an actual murder weapon but, if Mr de Ville is to be believed (and I currently choose to do so) the vast majority of the items he has shown me so far have dreadful associations; from a collar worn around the neck of a dog that hid under the expansive dress of Mary Queen of Scots at the very moment of her execution in February 1587 – a dog collar very different in type to my own – to a set of shirt studs worn by William Huskisson, the first victim of a fatal railway accident, in Darlington in September 1830.

'Why so much gloom and doom, Mr de Ville?' I finally feel I must ask. 'Surely you could sell objects with sunnier associations?'

'I only – er – acquire what I know that I, in turn, will be able to sell, Reverend Morris,' says the proprietor. 'I may find a customer for one of the original prisms fashioned and used by Isaac Newton to prove that sunlight is made up of many different colours of light, but such a man will be a specialist; a collector of scientific artefacts. On the other hand, it is human nature for most people to have a fascination with death, or close brushes with it. Take this, for example.' Mr de Ville turns and carefully lifts down something from a shelf behind him.

I look to see what he's holding. It's a small glass-lidded box containing what appear to be... *fingernails*?

Mr de Ville clearly enjoys my bafflement. 'They are fingernails from Admiral Lord Nelson's missing arm,' he explains. 'The one he had amputated after he was wounded in an attack on the Canary Islands in 1797.'

I cannot help but laugh. 'This is preposterous!' I snort. 'How can anyone hope to prove or disprove the origins of such an item?'

The proprietor of The Cabinet of Curiosities becomes suddenly stony-faced. 'I can personally guarantee the provenance of every single item I have shown you,' he says curtly. 'Of every single item in this shop. I would have thought that a man in your line of business would have *faith*.'

I suddenly feel a little uncomfortable, though it's hard to pinpoint exactly why. Perhaps I do not like the idea of his calling my vocation 'a business'. I realise that, despite having removed my coat sometime earlier, and de Ville having placed it on an ancient wooden stool (purportedly made from the wood of the tree from which Judas Iscariot hanged himself), I am now sweating profusely. Does he have a fire in another room, or some concealed system of heating?

'I really feel that it's time I was on my way, Mr de Ville,' I say, heading back through the maze of objects towards my coat. 'I have taken up enough of your time, especially when I have no plans to buy.'

'It really has been my pleasure, reverend,' says the proprietor, 'but, before you go, would you do me the honour of letting me show you one final item? My most recent acquisition?' He steps to one side to reveal an open doorway leading into a back room.

I feel guilty at my unease and readily agree. Mr de Ville has been nothing but polite, interesting and generous with his time since the moment I entered The Cabinet of Curiosities. I follow him into the back room to make amends. Small and windowless, it is even more hellishly hot than the main shop. It is empty, save for what must be the item that he wishes to show me.

Steeped in shadows is what looks very similar to an outsized Egyptian sarcophagus, but upright and made from iron. It is also free of ornamentation. There are no hieroglyphs, patterns or designs. It is strangely plain.

'What is this?' I ask. I know in the back of my mind that I've seen an illustration of something similar in a book.

'The secret of its fascinating function is revealed by studying it on the inside,' says Mr de Ville. Obscured in the shadows he swings the door – the lid – of the contraption open.

I step forward in the gloom, to study the lining... and grin. I know! This is one of those cabinets used by theatre magicians. I'm like a member of the audience invited up on stage to take part in a conjuring trick. This is more of Mr de Ville's magic, and I'm a part of it!

My pleasure turns to icy terror as I realise my ghastly mistake. I can feel the tips of row after row of metal spikes in my back. The great iron door is closing in on me. I'm too slow to move and there's no room to turn. I am done for. I can hear de Ville's laughter and, suddenly, all becomes clear.

God help me!

* * *

AN AFTERWORD

A small advertisement appears in *The London Clarion* some months after the events outlined in this story occur, stating that The Cabinet of Curiosities has recently acquired an iron maiden 'originally used as an instrument of torture during the Spanish

Inquisition' and that, unusually, it still contains 'the mortal remains of its final victim: a priest'. Its price is listed, as is the name of the proprietor. Possibly due to a typesetting error, Theo de Ville's name appears as 'The de Vil'.

DICK KING-SMITH

no place for frogs

ILLUSTRATIONS BY TONY ROSS

George Hoppitt was born in a rather dirty pond in Kent, not far
from Dover.

At first he was just one of two
thousand eggs his mother had laid.
Then he became a tadpole. Then he
became a proper little frog.

Strictly speaking, George was a Common Frog, but in fact, as
I shall tell you, he was a most uncommon one. At first he just
hopped about in the shallows of the pond with his many brothers
and sisters (not so many as there had been, because fish had
eaten a great many frogs' eggs and ducks had polished off an
awful lot of tadpoles).

But then one day there was a
very heavy summer rainstorm,
which soaked the ground around
the pond and, almost as though
someone had shouted, 'Go!',
George and all the rest scrambled
out of the pond into a jungle of
wet grass.

For the other froglets it was enough to hop about the nearby fields, but George was different. More than anything else he was curious, curious always to know what lay around the next corner. Alone of all the survivors of his mother's frogspawn, he set out on a journey; where to he did not know. For that matter he did not know that he was in Kent, or that he was not far from Dover, or that one day, after weeks of hard hopping over fields and across ditches and, occasionally, across roads, he would come to the top of some white cliffs.

George Hoppitt looked down and saw far below him not green grass, but golden sand. And beyond the sand was the sea!

George was amazed. *What an awful lot of water*, he thought. *Bit different from my old pond. I wonder what's on the other side of it?*

As he sat there gazing out, he heard a noise and looked round to see another frog, a big old frog.

'What's your name, sonny?' he croaked.

'George,' said George.

'Admiring the view, eh?' said the old frog.

'Yes,' replied George. 'Please, what's all that water?'

'That,' said the old frog, 'is the English Channel.'

'Oh. What's on the other side of it?'

'France.'

'Oh. Is that far?'

'About twenty miles.'

'Oh. Have you ever been there?'

'Not on your life, sonny!'

'Why not?'

'Because French people like frogs,' said the old one, and he hopped off.

Funny, thought George. *If they like us, that's a good reason for going there, isn't it? But how do I get down these cliffs?* He hopped a little way forward to have a look but he did one hop too many and tumbled over the edge.

However, George was not only a curious frog, he was also a lucky one, for the wind was blowing strongly up the face of the cliffs so he fell quite slowly, buoyed up by the sea breeze, twirling round and round, his arms and legs spread wide. Moreover, it was high tide, so that, instead of landing on rocks or on the beach, George fell with a small splash into the sea.

He looked back up at the white cliffs of Dover. *That's where I've come from*, he thought, *so France must be the opposite way*, and he turned around and began to swim. Not only was George a curious frog, not only a lucky frog, but a brave one, too, and he set out to cross the English Channel.

It was a long, long journey of course, which took him a whole day and night, and it did not help when, feeling thirsty, he took a gulp of sea water and found

that, unlike the water in his old pond, it was very salty.

Luckily there was a shower when he was about halfway across, so he lay on his back, opened his mouth and had a nice long drink of rainwater.

He was lucky, too, not to be run over by any of the many ships, big and small, that were sailing up or down the Channel, and he had some near misses! But as the sun rose on the morning of the second day, George saw land ahead.

Bravely he struggled on, till the tide took him and washed him ashore. Exhausted, George slept for a while on the sands of France, and then he hopped up the beach and into the nearest

patch of grass, which was wet with recent rain. *Just the place to meet a French frog*, George thought. *They like us, that old chap told me. I could make a pal.*

For a while George met nothing in the jungle of wet

grasses but French slugs and French worms and French beetles, all of which he ate greedily. But then, just as he was about to grab a particularly big worm, he heard a voice say, '*Fiche le camp!*' and looked round to see another big old frog, a French one this time of course.

'Sorry?' said George. 'What did you say?'

'*Ma foi!*' said the other. 'You are Engleesh?'

'Yes. I'm afraid I didn't understand what you said.'

'What I said,' replied the big old French frog, 'was... 'ow you say in Engleesh?... *un moment, mon petit*... ah, *oui*, I 'ave it... I said "Push off!" What ees an Engleesh *grenouille* doing in France? 'Ow you get 'ere?'

'I swam across the English Channel.'

'*Mon Dieu*! Why you do zis?'

'Someone told me that the French like frogs.'

The big old French frog began to shake with laughter. Out of his wide mouth came croaky chuckles and his pop-eyes filled with tears as he rocked about in mirth.

When at last he got his breath, he said, 'Eet is true, my Engleesh friend. Ze French do like frogs. To eat.'

'To eat?' cried George in horror.

'*Mais oui*. Not all of ze frog. Just ze legs,' said the big old

French frog, and he hopped away through the wet grass, still shaking with laughter.

As for George Hoppitt, as well as being curious and lucky and brave, he now became extremely scared. He stretched out each long leg in turn and imagined a Frenchman sinking his teeth into them, and then he turned and hopped back down the beach as fast as those long legs would propel him.

Into the Channel he went, turning his back on France, land of frog-eaters, and set out for England.

About halfway across George had a great stroke of luck.

A fishing boat came alongside him and one of the fishermen scooped him up with a net.

'Wotcher got there?' asked another of the crew.

'Flippin' frog. Trying to swim the flippin' Channel.'

'A French one, I expect. Doesn't want his legs to end up on a plate. Chuck 'im back.'

'Nah, nah, we'll give 'im a lift.'

They put George ashore at Dover and, brave, lucky and determined as he was, he set out for home, through the town, into the Kent countryside, until at last, many days and nights later, he reached that dirty old pond where he had been hatched.

Some of his brothers and sisters were still around and one of them said to him, 'Hullo, George. Haven't seen you around lately. Where've you been?'

'France.'

'France? Where's that?'

'Never you mind,' said George Hoppitt. 'It's no place for frogs.'

ROGER MCGOUGH

bubble trouble

ILLUSTRATION BY RIAN HUGHES

The trouble with Bobby is bubbles
Been his hobby since he was a boy
When Santa brought him a bubble
One Christmas instead of a toy .

Since then he has tried to recapture
The magic of that shimmering sphere
And decided the blowing of bubbles
Would be his chosen career

Fairy Liquid he pours on his cornflakes
Scented soap he spreads on his toast
To be undisputed world champion
'A billion I'll blow!' his proud boast

Golden globes, silver orbs and belishas
All manner of ball he creates
And with a fair wind behind him
A small zeppelin our hero inflates

But the trouble with all of his bubbles
Though perfect in every way
Though fashioned with love and attention
(And we're talking a thousand a day)

These incandescent flotillas
These gravitational blips
These would-be orbiting planets
Within seconds of leaving his lips

Go *POP!* Just like that.

MICHAEL MORPURGO

for carlos. a letter from your father

ILLUSTRATIONS BY MICHAEL FOREMAN

I have never forgotten my tenth birthday. All my other childhood birthdays are lost somewhere in the mists of memory, blurred by sameness perhaps: the excitement of anticipation, the brief rapture of opening presents and then the inevitable disappointment, because birthdays like Christmases were always so quickly over. Not so my tenth.

It is not only because of the gleaming silver bike my mother gave me that I remember it so well. I tried it out at once, in my pyjamas. In an ecstasy of joy and pride I rode it round and round the block, hoping all my friends would be up early and watching out of their windows, admiring, and seething with envy too. But even my memory of that has diminished over the years. It was when I came home, puffed out and glowing, and sat down for breakfast, that my mother gave me something else too. It is this second gift that I have never forgotten. I can't honestly remember what happened to my beautiful bike. Either it rusted away at the back of the garage when I grew out of it, or it was thrown away. I don't know. I do know that I still have this second gift, that I have never grown out of it, and that I will never throw it away.

She put down beside me on the kitchen table what looked at first like an ordinary birthday card. She didn't say who it was from, but I could see that there was something about this card that troubled her deeply.

'Who's it from?' I asked her. I wasn't that interested at first – after all birthday cards were never as intriguing as presents. She didn't answer me. I picked up the envelope. There, written in handwriting I did not know, was my answer: 'For Carlos. A letter from your Father.'

The envelope had clearly been folded. It was soiled and there was a tear in one corner. The word 'Father' was smeared and only just legible. I looked up and saw my mother's eyes filled with tears. I knew instantly she wanted me to ask no more questions. She simply said, 'He wanted me to keep it for you, until your tenth birthday.' So I opened the letter and read:

Dearest Carlos,

I want to wish you first of all a very happy tenth
birthday. How I should love to be with you on this
special day. Maybe we could have gone riding together as
I once did with my father on my birthday. Was it *my*
tenth? I can't remember. I do remember we rode all day
and picnicked on a high hill where the wind breathed
through the long grass. I thought I could see for ever
from that hill. Or maybe we could have gone to a football
match and howled together at the referee and leaped up
and down when we scored.

But then maybe you don't like horses or football. Why
should you have grown up like me? You are a different
person, but with a little of me inside you, that's all. I do
know that your mother and I would have sung *Happy
Birthday* to you and watched your eyes light up when you
opened your presents, and as you blew out the candles on
your cake.

But all I have to give, all I can offer is this letter, a
letter I hope you will never have to read, for if you are
reading it now it means that I am not with you, and have
never been with you, that I died ten years ago in some
stupid, stupid war that killed me and many, many others,
and like all wars did no one any good.

Death, Carlos, as you know, comes to each of us.
Strangely, I am not afraid, not as much as I have been. I

think maybe that love has conquered my fear. I am filled with so much love for you, and such a sadness too, a sadness I pray you will never have to know. It is the thought of losing you before I even get to know you that saddens me so. If I die in this terrible place then we shall never meet, not properly, father to son. We shall never talk. For a father to be parted from his son is always a terrible thing, yet if it has to be, then in a way I would rather it was now, this way, this soon. To have known you, to have watched you grow and then to have lost you must surely be even worse. Or am I just telling myself that?

You will know me a little I suppose, perhaps from photographs. And your mother may well have told you something about me, of my childhood, how I grew up on the farm in Patagonia and was riding horses almost before I could walk. Maybe she told you of our first meeting when her car had a puncture and I was riding by and stopped to change her wheel for her. I'm quite good at tinkering with motors – you have to be on a farm. But I took a lot longer to change that wheel than I needed to – if you know what I mean. By the time I had finished I knew I loved her and I wanted to spend my whole life with her. Later I learned that she went home afterwards and told her sister that she'd met this young man on the road who had nice eyes and a nice horse, but who talked too much and was hopeless at changing wheels. Anyway, much against the wishes of our families, who all said we were far too young, we got married six months later.

For a short while life seemed so sweet, so perfect. Then came my conscription papers, and separation, and the long weeks of military training. But I didn't mind that much because it was something we all had to do and because I knew it would soon be over. I had so much to look forward to, most of all the birth of you. All the talk in the barracks was of war. I think we talked ourselves into this war – perhaps it is always like that.

I came home to see you just once, and now, only a few weeks later, I find myself sitting here in the Malvinas, high in the rocky hills above Stanley Town. Night is coming on and I am waiting for battle. As I write this I am so cold I cannot feel my feet. I can hardly hold the pencil I am writing with. The British are coming. They know where we are. They have been bombarding us all day. We cannot see them, but we know they are out there somewhere. We expect them to attack tonight. All of us know in our hearts, though we do not say it, that this will be the last battle. In battle, men die. I do not want to think of that, but it is difficult not to. The officers say we can win, that if we can only hang on reinforcements will soon be here. But we all know better. They have to say that, don't they?

I can see you now in my head, as you were three long
months ago on the morning I left home. When I looked
down upon you that last time, cradled in your mother's
arms, I remember I tried to picture you as a grown boy.
I couldn't then and I still can't. For me you are that
sleeping child, yawning toothlessly, fists clenched,
frowning through your milk-soaked dreams. But grow up
you will, grow up you have, and now that you are old
enough I want to tell you myself how I came to be here
fighting a war in this dreadful place, how I died so far
from home. I want to speak to you directly. At least you
will know me a little because you can hear my voice in
my writing. It is true that I am writing to you also
because it helps me – if I think of you I do not think of
the battle ahead. I have already written to your mother.
She will have read her letter ten years ago now. This is
your letter, Carlos, our hello you might call it, and our
goodbye.

I had not thought it would end like this. Like all my
comrades I believed in what we were told, in what we
saw on the television, in what we read in the papers. The
Malvinas belonged to Argentina, and that much is true.
They had been stolen from us, they said. We would
restore the honour of Argentina and take them back. Our
flag would fly again over Stanley. It would be easy, they
told us. We would attack in force, overwhelm the British

garrison in a few hours. There would be very little shooting. The Malvinas would be ours again, Argentinian, and then we could all go home. I was excited – we all were, excited and proud, too, proud that we were the ones chosen to do this for our country. It was all going to be so simple.

And it began well. We came ashore in our landing craft. No one fired a shot at us. As we marched into Stanley we saw our flag already flying high over the town. The British marines in their green berets sat huddled by the roadside, dejected, defeated. The war was over almost before it had begun. Or so we thought. We had won. The Malvinas were ours again. How the people back home would be cheering, I thought. What heroes we would be when we returned. How we laughed and sang and drank that first night. We did not feel the cold in the wind, not then. In those early days on the Malvinas, in that first flush of victory, the islands seemed to us like a paradise, a paradise regained. Our paradise. Argentinian.

Yet here I sit only a month or two later and we know that we are about to lose the last battle. The ships did not come. The supplies did not come. Instead the British came, their planes first, then their ships, then their soldiers. We did what we could, Carlos, but we were raw conscripts, poorly fed, poorly equipped, badly led and we

for carlos. a letter from your father

were up against determined fighters. From the moment they sunk the great battleship *Belgrano*, the pride of our navy, we knew it could only end one way – I lost my cousin in that ship. I saw men die, good men, my friends, men with wives and mothers and children.

I grew up fast in the terrible weeks that followed. I learned what I should already have understood, that in wars people really do kill one another. I did not hate those I killed, and those who try to kill me do not hate me either. We are like puppets doing a dance of death, our masters pulling the strings, watched by the world on television. What they don't know is that the puppets are made of flesh, not wood. War, Carlos, has only one result: suffering.

When I heard the British had landed at San Carlos Bay, I thought of you, and I prayed in the church in Stanley that I would be spared to see you again. They had no candles there. So I went out and bought a box of candles from the store and then I came back and lit them and prayed for me, for you, for your mother. An old lady in a scarf was kneeling at prayer. I saw her watching me as I came away. Her eyes met mine and she tried to smile. My English is not that good, but I remember her words. They echo still in my head.

'This is not the way,' she said. 'It is wrong, wrong.'

'Yes,' I replied, and left her there.

That was a few days ago now. Since then we have been stuck up here on these freezing hills above Stanley Town, digging in and waiting for the British, who come closer every day. And the terrible wind, from which we cannot hide, chills us to the bone, sapping the last of our strength and most of our courage too. What courage we have left we shall fight with, but courage will not be enough.

I must finish now. I must fold you away in an envelope, and face whatever I must face. As you grow up, you may not have had a father, but I promise you, you have always had a father's love.

Goodbye Carlos. And God bless.

Papa

DEBORAH WRIGHT

the amazing furniture zoo park

ILLUSTRATIONS BY CHRIS MOULD

Tristan woke up on the morning of his seventh birthday feeling rather miserable. He glanced down at the bottom of his bed. It was unlikely that his parents had bought him any presents, since they'd forgotten for the last seven years running, but he could always hope.

His heart leapt. There *was* something at the bottom of his bed. It looked like a card.

It was made out of a folded piece of toilet paper. Tristan opened it up and sighed. Inside, it said: HAPPY BIRTHDAY TOM! They hadn't even managed to get his name right.

As you might have guessed by now, Tristan's parents weren't exactly wonderful people.

The trouble was, they were both much too much in love with money to care about their only son. They both worked all of the day and most of the night in a large bank in London. They were very stingy when it came to

pocket money; Tristan only got one pence a week and if he was bad, it often went into minus numbers, which was charged at a rate of twenty-five per cent interest.

Tristan got dressed and went downstairs, hoping he might, just might, have *one* tiny little present.

'Presents!' his mother cried. She was standing behind an ironing board, frantically rubbing her iron over some crumpled fifty-pound notes to make them smooth and crisp. 'I can't talk now, I'm too busy! Ask your father.'

'Presents!' his father cried. He was standing in the kitchen, lightly grilling a five-pound note. His father loved money so much he liked to eat it; he said it tasted much nicer than toast. 'Now look what you've made me do!' he cried as the note burst into flames. 'You distracted me! Your pocket money this month is now minus fifty-seven pounds, and 3.0005000 pence!'

'Thanks,' said Tristan sullenly. 'Oh, and by the way,' he added, 'my name is Tristan. Not Tom. You got my birthday card wrong.'

'That's another fifty pence off for being cheeky,' his father blustered.

'*Dad, that's not fair!*' Tristan cried.

'Shut up!' said his mother, storming into the kitchen. 'Your father and I are late for work. Now you can do something useful and spend the day reading the *Financial Times* and deciding which shares you'd buy – if you ever manage to earn any money.'

As his parents zoomed off to work, Tristan trudged up to his bedroom and sat by the window, feeling rather miserable. The clouds were grey and grumpy and it was just starting to rain. It wasn't going to be much of a fun day, just sitting and watching the rain form watery spiders' webs across the glass.

To cheer himself up, Tristan sank into his favourite fantasy daydream. He was a superhero, battling against villains and saving people's lives (especially beautiful young girls). He was just about to do battle with an alien spaceship when—

—suddenly the doorbell rang. Tristan's heart leapt. But it sank pretty quickly when he glanced down and saw who it was: his mad Uncle Max.

Tristan didn't like his Uncle Max very much. He was old and had a hoary grey beard and smelt of Bovril and, most of all, he was completely bonkers. Unfortunately, before Tristan could hide, his uncle looked up and spotted him.

'AHA!' he shouted. 'DON'T TRY TO HIDE, YOU IMPUDENT BOY! I'M COMING UP TO GET YOU!'

And then his uncle did something that made Tristan gawp in amazement. He opened up his large green umbrella and sailed up to the window.

'Come on, birthday boy,' he said, grabbing hold of Tristan with one hand whilst hanging on to the extraordinary umbrella with the other. 'We're going out for the day. We're going to the zoo! Come on, Umbrella!'

'All right, all right,' a female voice came from nowhere.

When Tristan looked down, he felt his stomach lurch. He closed his eyes and hung on tightly as they swung into a large froth of cloud.

Well, he thought to himself, *this is all pretty strange. Still, it is much more fun than staying at home and reading about shares...*

When he opened his eyes, the clouds had parted and they were sailing to the ground. It was then that Tristan realised this was no ordinary zoo. There was a large pink neon sign outside that blazed: MAD UNCLE MAX'S AMAZING FURNITURE ZOO PARK.

'*Furniture* zoo park?' Tristan asked. 'Isn't that bit weird?'

'You must be weird to think it's weird,' said Uncle Max. 'Now come on, you impudent boy. We don't have to queue, since I own the zoo. We can go right on in.'

He folded his umbrella, ignoring her squeak-shrieks of protest and tucked her under his arm.

Inside the zoo, they walked up to the first cage. It was filled with tall green trees and bushes. A few large slabs of pink meat, oozing juice, were lying on the grass. There were signs plastered all over the cages saying: DANGER! DO NOT TOUCH THE FENCE! YOU MAY BE BITTEN!

A crowd had gathered round. People were pointing and whispering nervously. Tristan frowned.

'What's in it?' he asked his uncle.

'Can't you see?' his uncle whispered, pointing.

Yes, he could see *something*... behind those trees... a flash of pink...

All of a sudden a large pink flowery sofa jumped out from behind the trees. It munched some grass, growling uneasily at the crowds.

Tristan started to laugh, but his uncle gave him a stern look, so he quickly shut up.

'Look,' said his uncle.

Tristan looked. Something blue was flashing behind the trees...

Another sofa!

This was one was blue with white stripes. It seemed to be creeping up behind the pink sofa...

The pink sofa hadn't noticed...

'Ooh,' the crowd gasped. A little boy started to cling to his father's leg and whimper in terror. Even Tristan couldn't help feeling a little afraid. The sofa *did* look fierce, pausing and sniffing the wind, seeming to sense that it was being watched.

'Look out,' Tristan whispered, his heart beating.

Crash! The blue sofa pounced on to the pink one. The pink one fell on its side, looking surprised and dazed. The blue one knocked it again, buffeting it with big, hard blows.

'Fight! Fight! Fight!' Uncle Max cried in excitement, roaring with laughter as the two sofas started to tussle with each other, rolling over and over in the grass.

'What's that!?' Tristan cried, seeing something yellow and fluffy on the grass.

Then he realised it was stuffing. There was a large gash in the side of the pink sofa and the stuffing was pouring out.

'My sofas!' Uncle Max rattled the cage. 'Don't let them kill each other!'

A zoo keeper quickly jumped up and hosed a stream of water on to them. They leapt apart, sopping wet, growling rather grumpily. The crowds moved on, looking nervous.

Tristan turned to his uncle.

'That was amazing!' he cried. 'But are they alive? Or are they robots?'

'Robots! Of course not! Just because you can move around, do people ask you if you're a robot? No they don't, you rude child! Listen, all furniture is alive. The furniture sitting back in your home right now is alive.'

'What?' Tristan really thought that Uncle Max had gone completely and utterly bonkers now; his brain cells had clearly fallen out in the night and were lying at home on his pillow.

'Are you trying to say,' Tristan asked, 'that my bed and the table and the TV and the mixer in the kitchen and the oven and... and... all those things are alive?'

'Exactly. They're very crafty creatures. They're so clever that they can sit still all day without moving. But the next time you're home, take a very close look at your sofa or TV – you'll see just a very slight movement. They have to move a millimetre or so because they're breathing.'

'Oh really?' said Tristan doubtfully. Because deep down inside he still didn't quite believe him. The idea was simply preposterous. But then again, so was a green umbrella that flew and talked.

'Now come on, on we go – we have to go to the exotic house now.'

As they left, Tristan had a funny feeling that something was wrong. But his uncle was walking ahead at such a brisk pace that Tristan ignored his heart and hurried on.

They continued their tour of the zoo and saw all kinds of weird and wonderful creatures. They had photographs taken with cushions on their laps and curtains draped round their shoulders (which was quite difficult when the curtains kept hissing and slithering off).

'Here,' said his uncle, passing him a pink curtain with a slightly shy smile, 'you can keep one to take home. Don't forget to feed it, mind. It needs three large curtain hooks a day.'

'Er, thanks,' said Tristan, draping it over his arm. It wasn't quite the pet he'd always dreamed of, but he was touched by his uncle's kindness.

They saw food mixers in glass cages playfully throwing liquidised fruit over each other. Once, Tristan even glanced up and saw knives and forks flying overhead, migrating to countries where they would be used to eat warmer foods.

They came to an enclosure with a large turquoise pool. A keeper held out a pair of fish and then – *whoosh!* – a pair of Hoovers came flying up out of the water, snapping up the fish in their metal jaws. A few seconds later, their dust bags were filled with silvery bones and they vroom-vroomed hungrily for more.

Lastly, they came to a cage filled with Walkmans and hi-fis. A keeper was trying to remove the hi-fis' aerials, wincing as they emitted fuzzy little squeals of pain.

'They're being neutered,' Uncle Max explained. 'They breed like rabbits otherwise!'

'Is it safe to put Walkmans and hi-fis together?' Tristan asked nervously. 'Don't they fight each other?'

'Don't be stupid,' said his uncle. 'Everyone knows that Walkmans grow up to be radios – what do they teach you in school these days?'

Tristan noticed that batteries kept falling out of the walkmans and thudding to the floor.

'Won't they go flat?' he asked.

'Run flat? As I've told you before, they're not robots, they're alive. No, it's poo!'

'Poo?' Tristan asked in disbelief. 'Poo?'

'People are very polite in England so they call them batteries. Unfortunately, they've got diarrhoea at the moment, because they've been playing too many Westlife albums – enough to make anyone feel ill, I should think. Ah,' he checked his watch. 'Goodness me, how the day has flown. Time to go home I think...'

He was about to send Tristan off with a pat on the head and a jar of Bovril, when he heard a sudden growling noise behind him.

'LOOK OUT!' Tristan cried.

But it was too late. His uncle turned in bewilderment as the blue and white striped sofa that had been hovering in the shadows behind them, finally pounced.

Tristan gasped as it flung its cushions against his uncle's head, battering him to the ground. *It must have escaped from its cage*, he realised. *Oh dear God, I knew there was something wrong; the cage wasn't locked properly, if only I'd said something.*

His uncle had now disappeared under the sofa, which was making guzzling sounds. What could he do? What could he do?

'Here boy, here,' Tristan tried to whistle, but the sofa seemed too busy enjoying gobbling up his uncle.

Then, as he gazed down at his arm, inspiration struck. He picked up the pink curtain and waved it temptingly.

The sofa paused and let out an *mmmmmmm-that-looks-yummy* noise. Then he lunged at the curtain.

Tristan started to run, waving the curtain (the poor thing was shrieking in terror) as the sofa came after him in hot pursuit. He felt its flowery hem snapping at his heels and his heart started to hammer. He was nearly there, nearly there.

He rounded the corner – and *wham*! – the waiting keepers held open the cage door. Tristan darted aside and the sofa went skidding back into its cage. The keepers burst into a round of applause. One of them took the whimpering curtain away, gently stroking it better.

'Well, thank goodness for my brilliant nephew!' his uncle cried, staggering to his feet and slapping a meaty hand on Tristan's shoulder. 'You, my dear boy, are a real hero.'

Though Tristan had always fantasised about fighting aliens rather than sofas, he couldn't help a glow of pride sweeping over him. He looked up at his uncle and decided that, despite the fact that he was old and had a hoary grey beard and was totally bonkers, he really rather liked him.

Uncle Max looked down at Tristan and smiled back.

'You can come back anytime to the zoo. I'll give you a season ticket. Then, whenever you're bored, just think of me and I'll pop up with the umbrella.'

'Thanks,' said Tristan gratefully. 'I'd like that very much.'

Back home, Tristan felt rather happy. It had been the best birthday he'd had in a long time, even if it had been rather strange.

He was so tired after so much excitement that he collapsed on to the sofa and fell into a deep sleep. When he woke up several hours later, the day's adventures suddenly flashed before him. He sat up and gazed around the living room in awe. Could the furniture really be alive?

Tristan jiggled up and down on the sofa. Nothing happened. He tiptoed up to the TV and tweaked the aerial. Nothing happened.

I'm being stupid, thought Tristan. *Soon people will be calling me Mad Nephew Tristan. Of course it isn't alive. This is the real world and the furniture zoo was just a dream...*

And then he heard a noise. It came from the sofa, and it seemed as though the sofa was reminding him of what the reality was...

It sounded – if he listened very hard – like a long, low, snarling growl...

Tristan smiled wickedly and sat down, waiting for his parents to come home.

GEORGIA BYNG

racing guinea pigs

ILLUSTRATIONS BY RUSSELL AYTO

This is a brilliant game to play with your friends but also a great game to bet on, and so it is good for fêtes or other money-raising events.

You will need:

A guinea pig

10 identical boxes

A load of old cardboard

Tape

A pen

Scissors

One special cardboard box for the guinea pig

Preparation

At all costs treat your guinea pig with great respect! If anyone is too loud or excited, and frightening your guinea pig, put him in his special box. Remember your guinea pig is the star of this show and must be given first-class treatment. He will need to be fit and happy to perform if anyone is to win. Not all guinea pigs are racers, but most of them are.

Set up the game by taking your ten identical boxes and number them 1-10, writing the numbers on the side. Place the boxes in a ring, with the open part of the box facing towards the middle. You now have ten guinea pig shelters. Put the boxes close to each other so that your racing guinea pig cannot squeeze between them. With the cardboard, make a barrier around the outside of the boxes, so that should your guinea pig charge between the boxes, he won't escape entirely.

Betting

Each person bets on a box. You can bet with sweets or money. If you are playing for money, charge whatever you like for a box, but I suggest £1 a box if you are trying to raise money for charity. Make sure you sell all ten boxes before you start the race. At £1 a box you should collect £10. The prize money, which you take from this £10, should be £5. That leaves you £5 profit for your charity each time the race is run. Have two million races and you make a million pounds, but that would take years. If you run twenty races you make £100. So that's pretty good.

Winning

So, how does someone win the prize money? Easy. This is how...
When everyone is set for the start of the race, they each stand behind the box they have bought. The rules are that people must not come over the outside barrier, or touch the guinea pig. Nor must anyone attempt to stop the guinea pig from going in the

direction that he chooses. The players may wave and make gentle noises of encouragement, but no shooing with magazines or nasty stuff like that. When the guinea pig enters a box fully, the 'owner' of that box has won.

Racing

Now the race is ready to start. Bring your guinea pig over to the arena. Tell him what a handsome fellow he is, the best looking guinea pig on the planet, that sort of thing. Build his confidence up. Now, carefully put him down in the centre of the ring with the special cardboard box over him. When everyone is ready, he's under starter's orders...

Lift the box and he's off...

He'll scurry forward, change his mind, shoot off in one direction and then in another. He may investigate one or two boxes. Eventually he will chose a box to go in to. Only when the guinea pig's tail has gone right over the threshold of a box and his body is inside it too, has that box won.

Have fun, but most of all, make sure that your guinea pig does.

Finally

This game can be played with two guinea pigs in each race, you just have to split the prize money. Also, I am sure that hamsters, rats, rabbits and mice are good racers too, but I think guinea pigs are the best because guinea pigs squeak.

GERALDINE MCCAUGHREAN

sky ship

ILLUSTRATIONS BY TIM STEVENS

We look down into the
sea and think of
mermaids looking up
at us – looking up at
a surface mottled
with sunlight. But, if
you think about it, we
are like the mermaids.
We too have a
ceiling of blue
overhanging
our heads. True, it is
higher than the tallest building – but then
parts of the ocean are countless storeys
deep. Just suppose that we too live in a kind
of an ocean – an ocean of air – and that above us glitters and shifts
the sunlit blue of yet another sea – a sea-in-the-sky. There was a time
when our ancestors believed it – believed that the rain leaked out of
that freshwater ocean, through imperfections in the baggy clouds; that
our birds were the fishes of that upper ocean. What is more, they

believed that ships sailed on that upper ocean, crewed by skymen and skymaids. Once or twice in the long history of incredible events, the two worlds even met.

One dankly overcast Sunday morning in the year of 1214, people came spilling out of church, yawning and stretching themselves after a two-hour sermon. They were just turning for home when a sudden clang and a sprinkling of stone dust made them look up. Something had struck the church tower. CLANG. BANG. It was still there, jarring against the stonework, chipping the waterspouts.

An anchor.

Its flukes scraped off birdlime and prised out mortar. Then, just as it seemed about to swing clear, it twirled once more in mid-air and snagged a window halfway up the tower.

The anchor cable, reaching up and away, far out of sight, twanged taut and a noise of groaning timbers came from beyond the clouds. There were shouts, too, and no mistaking the anger and confusion in the voices, though the language was like none spoken on Earth.

The vicar was worried about the damage to his church, but the rest of the congregation stood spellbound, gazing upwards, as unseen hands tugged to free the snagged anchor of an unseen ship. At every tug, the anchor writhed in the window, but only wedged itself more tightly than ever. Suddenly Jack, standing among the gravestones with his father, pointed upwards and shouted, 'Look there! A foot!' And someone else cried, 'A man!'

Through the low cloud and down the rope came a sailor,

climbing hand-over-hand. His cheeks a-bulge, his eyes screwed almost shut, he clambered down the anchor cable, holding his breath. Jack's father, Caleb, shook his head in sympathy. He was a sailor and he, too, in his time, had been sent over the side of a ship to free a snagged anchor. As he told Jack, 'When a captain needs dangerous work doing, a sailor's life is cheap.'

Redder and redder the man's face grew, bluer and bluer the veins in his throat. His foot caught the wind vane. The brittle metal snagged the cloth of his trousers and, as he struggled to pull free, the anchor cable wrapped itself around him and he, like the anchor, was snagged.

'He's drowning!' yelled Jack. The crowd boggled at him. Foolish boy. How could a man drown in the fresh air?

'He's right!' exclaimed Caleb. 'His kind don't breathe air!'

Then ten sets of feet were pounding up the tower stairs, setting the rungs rattling, setting the church booming with echoes. The anchor, jutting in at the window, blocked their path. They wrestled to free it, but it was wedged fast. By the time they squirmed past and reached the roof, the poor matelot lay gasping on the parapet three-quarters dead from drowning.

Quick as a whip, Caleb and his son Jack snatched out their knives and began sawing at the rope. Aboard the sky ship someone shouted a muffled command. The words were strange but the meaning was plain as day to Caleb. 'Captain's calling for an axe to cut free the anchor.'

'What? With his own man still down here?' Jack was horrified. He sawed at the rope so hard that his fingers began to blister.

Caleb pulled a face. 'He has to put the life of his ship above the life of one man. This one's only a sailor, after all, isn't he? Only a sailor, like me.' Strand by strand they hacked through the thick anchor cable. Above their heads the captain's cries became more angry and more urgent. Perhaps the crew of the sky ship was purposely slow in fetching the axe – thinking of the comrade they would cut loose, along with the anchor. Even so, what tide-rips or wild waves were battering the sky ship, pinioned as she was by her own anchor, unable to break free.

'I'm nearly through!' cried Jack, and Caleb threw his knife

aside and lashed the drowning man to the anchor cable using his own belt. Before the knot was even tight, Jack cut the last strand of rope and the sky sailor was lugged skywards between them, like a puppet jerked offstage by its puppeteer. Unseen hands aboard the unseen ship were hauling in both cable and man.

'*I'm going up there*! I'm going to see the sea in the sky!' cried Jack. He jumped on to the parapet and caught hold of the rope. To have caught a glimpse of another world and to let it slip through his fingers was more than Jack could bear. But, as he swung into the air, his father grabbed him by the legs. 'Let go, Father! I must see what's up there!'

'*Help me*!' cried Caleb, and the sexton and the carpenter and the vicar all stumbled across the roof and grabbed hold of Jack's legs as the sky ship's anchor chain swept him away. With four grown men dragging on his legs, it was impossible for Jack to hold on. With a sob of frustration and despair, he dropped back down on to the tower roof, clamping his hands under his armpits to ease the pain of the rope burns. '*You should have let me go*!' he raged. 'You should have let me see that sky ship! I would have been the first! No one has ever seen... what's up there.'

Caleb sank his fingers in his son's damp air. 'And do you know what would have happened if you had gone? Do you? Do you? The very next cloudburst would have dropped you down dead at your mother's feet like a drowned kitten. *Think,* boy! You can't breathe sky water, any more than they can breathe our air! Let it go, son. Let it go.'

And they stood watching – like mermaids on a reef – as the clouds above their heads buckled and bulged, and the unseen ship set an unknown course across the ocean-in-the-sky.

For many years, the anchor stayed wedged in the church tower window, a tantalising souvenir of an encounter with an alien race of men. The vicar (who discouraged such talk) told visitors that it dated back to a hurricane, a great tempest, when cows and carts and ships and anchors were blown into the treetops and left hanging from the spires. But his congregation knew better. Wonders such as that cannot be glossed over.

As for Jack, he took to watching the swallows swoop and glide in shoals through the higher reaches of the sky. And when, like his father, he became a sailor, he would often astound his fellow crew by climbing to the mainmast top, to be closer to the sky. He was always hoping, he said, to glimpse a keel, a whale, a swimmer, a raft afloat in the sea above him.

The incident of the sky ship was recorded by Gervaise of Tilbury who, despite his name, lived in Arles, France in the thirteenth century, and took a lifelong interest in witches and the supernatural.

JEREMY STRONG

this is NOT a fairy tale

ILLUSTRATIONS BY CLARE MACKIE

This is something that happened a long time
ago, before history began, before people
knew what was real and what wasn't –
although they *thought* they knew the
difference. It was a
time when bears
and wolves
roamed the
countryside, when
there were trolls and
goblins, dwarves and
unicorns, dragons and witches and wicked
stepmothers and proud queens who were not as beautiful as
Snow White, and so on... You get the picture.

Luke was a young man of eighteen. He was good-looking, but
very poor. His father had died when a pig fell on him. (That was
the sort of accidental death people had in those days. Luke's
grandmother had been mown down by a flock of runaway

chickens.) Luke was only six when his father died, and after that he was brought up by his mother, Old Crone, and his pet dog, Shaggy.

There was little work to be found in the ramshackle village where Luke lived and because there was little work there was no money to be made. Luke made do as best he could. He was happy to turn his hand to anything, so he did a bit of wood chopping here and a bit of shepherding there and so on. In this way he just about managed to keep himself fed, although his clothes would certainly not have won any fashion prizes. They were torn and tattered and dirty.

Luke did, however, have one big advantage despite his humble environment. He had a brain, and Luke's brain was a good brain and he used it for doing what brains do best of all – thinking. He used to listen to what all the wise old villagers used to chat about during the long dark evenings. He would lap up every word. He would listen to their old tales, enthralled.

The old villagers were very proud of their wisdom. They would sit round a winter fire and say things like: 'We be wise old villagers. What I say is, before the last apple falls, there'll be trouble.'

And all the other elders of the village would go: 'Ooh, ahh, Old Jezebel, she be right there. Before the last apple falls, there'll be trouble!'

And then someone else might say: 'Ah, but when the moon is red and the hawthorn is in bloom, that's the time to be darning socks!' And they would all nod their heads in agreement.

Luke would listen to all this ancient wisdom and he soon came to the conclusion that it was mostly a load of nonsense. He worked out that if he lived his life based on the things the elders told him he would never get anything done at all. He certainly was not going to wait for a red moon and blooming hawthorn before he set about darning *his* socks. He decided to use his own brain instead.

Now, it so happened that there was a lot of talk in the village about the local princess. Her name was Ramona and she lived at the top of the mountain. (The village was at the bottom.) It was said that Ramona had flaming-red hair and was as beautiful as the sunset. Very few people had actually seen the princess because she had never come down from the mountain, and they had never been up it. The only way people knew about her was because occasionally messages were sent down from the castle. They were written on paper, folded into darts and launched over the battlements.

Ramona was due for marriage, but despite the best efforts of her parents, no suitable husband could be found. The rules for marriage were the usual weird rules that people used in those days. The prospective suitor had to climb the mountain from bottom to top and then he could claim the hand of the gorgeous

Ramona. You may think there was little that was difficult about this, and you would be right to think that actually climbing the mountain – the climbing bit itself – was not terribly difficult.

No, the awkward bit was what might happen on the way. You see, as you went up the mountain you would quite likely meet with the Black Bear. If you didn't see *him* you would no doubt come across the Trolls of Tiddly Crag, or the Waggletooth Witch. Then there were the Wild Wolves of Black Fen, the Dragon of Doom and – most frightening of all – the Giant Man-Eating Unicorn That Nobody Had Ever Seen. So all the suitors died on their way up, and this was also why Ramona never came down from the castle and all messages were sent down by paper dart.

(You may wish to know how the villagers got messages up to the castle and the short answer is, they didn't. They had yet to invent a dart that could be flung that high.)

Now Luke was not only bright, he was adventurous. Nowadays he would have gone white-water rafting and bungee jumping, but nobody had heard of such things in those days, so he didn't. But he did want to see the world. He wanted to escape from the humdrum little village where half of the elders spouted nonsense. He wanted to travel, but he didn't want to do it by himself. He wanted a companion. So it was that his thoughts turned towards the Princess Ramona.

Luke knew all about the dreadful creatures that haunted the mountain, yet he was still determined to see if he could win the hand of the beautiful Princess Ramona in marriage. He sat down and had a long, hard think. Then he got up and packed his bag. He put in some fruit, a sandwich and a salami sausage for the journey, because he didn't know how long it would take, and he set off up the mountain.

As he left the village the elders shouted after him: 'If you see the Waggletooth Witch you must cross your fingers behind your back and run like the wind and shout out the alphabet backwards!'

Some of them offered this advice too: 'When the Black Bear tries to eat you, rub your skin with acorn juice and hiss. Then the bear will vanish.'

Even his mother had wise words for him: 'Trolls love to dance. If you come across them you must play your magic violin and they will dance and dance until they drop down dead.'

'Right,' nodded Luke. He told everyone that he would certainly bear in mind their advice and he set off. He had not got far before he came across a patch of brambles as big as Europe. The brambles were thick and tall and covered in sharp, flesh-tearing thorns. What made them worse was that here and there he could see bits of torn clothing left behind by some of the princes who had tried to find a way through. There were  even a few skeletons hanging around. They didn't look very happy.

Luke looked at the brambles and he thought for a bit and then he made himself a small fire. He found two nice bits of thick wood and pushed their ends into the fire and waited until they had caught the flame nicely. Armed with these flaming brands Luke advanced on the brambles. They sizzled and hissed and spat and curled up and shrivelled at the heat from the flames and so, bit by bit, Luke made his way through the brambles, leaving a nice, clean, charred path behind him, ready for his return.

Luke pressed on up the mountain, whistling. All of a sudden out popped the Waggletooth Witch. She was hairy, she was horrid. She was the ugliest thing Luke had ever laid eyes on. Her nose was like a giant parrot's beak, but covered with warts and pimples and sprouting hairs. Did Luke cross his fingers behind his back and run away saying the alphabet backwards? No.

'I'm going to put a nasty spell on you!' cackled the witch.

'Why's that?' asked Luke, quite reasonably.

'Because I am so hideous and you are so handsome I cannot bear the sight of you.' And the witch reached into her handbag and pulled out her wicked witch's wand.

'I don't know why you say you are hideous,' said Luke, calmly. 'I think you are extraordinary.'

The witch, who was just in the process of making all the right sort of wavy movements with her wand before casting the spell, stopped in mid-wave. 'What? Why do you say that?'

Luke boldly stepped forward. He didn't want to show how frightened he was. 'Oh yes, you really are quite extraordinary. I have never seen a nose like yours. It is unique. It is wonderful.'

The Waggletooth Witch blushed. She did! She turned pink and then red and then back to pink. She fluttered her eyelashes. 'Oh you! You're just saying that!'

(Luke was thinking: *Of course I'm saying that. You couldn't hear me if I weren't.* But he kept his thoughts to himself, which is always a wise thing to do at times such as this.)

'It's true,' said Luke.

'Ah, well I am not sure I believe you,' said the Waggletooth Witch with a cunning leer. 'I bet you wouldn't dare kiss me.'

Luke smiled. (Behind the smile his teeth were firmly gritted.) 'I thought you'd never ask,' he said, and he gave the witch a stonking kiss.

To say that the Waggletooth Witch was amazed would be an understatement. She staggered back, quite delighted. Nobody had ever kissed her before, not even her own mother when she was a child. 'What a perfect gentleman you are. Nobody has ever done that to me. I wish you luck on your journey.'

And Luke carried on up the mountain, thinking that a little

kindness often went a long way. All at once the bushes parted and out sprang the Black Bear. Did Luke rub himself with acorn juice and hiss? No, he didn't.

'Grrrr,' said the bear, in a bearish sort of way. 'What are you doing halfway up this mountain?'

'I have come to seek the hand of the Princess Ramona,' explained Luke.

'Oh really? Do you know how many princes I have eaten?'

'No, I don't,' Luke answered truthfully.

'Thirty-two,' said the bear, also truthfully.

'Then you must have been very hungry,' Luke replied, and that stopped the bear in his tracks. The bear had never heard the like. Of course he had been hungry. That was why he ate all the princes.

Luke sat down at the bear's feet and patted the grass beside him. 'In my bag I have some salami. Would you like some?'

'What is salami?' asked the bear, sitting down and gazing at Luke with great curiosity.

Luke got out the salami sausage and he let the bear smell it. Then he cut off a big chunk and gave it to the bear. The Black Bear ate the salami and licked his lips and said he thought that salami sausage was a lot nicer than princes and a lot less bony. Then he wished Luke good luck with his journey and hoped that they would meet again.

Luke carried on up the mountain and before long he came face to face with the Trolls of Tiddly Crag. *What a busy day I'm having,* thought Luke. The trolls surrounded Luke and danced round him chanting horrible things. They were short, ugly little creatures, with needle-sharp teeth and a taste for human flesh. Now they bared their teeth and pulled horrible faces at Luke.

Did Luke pull out his magic violin and make them dance until they all dropped down dead? Of course not. He didn't have a magic violin and he didn't know how to play the violin even if he *did* have one.

Instead he just stood there and laughed. 'You're so cute!' he told the trolls.

'No we're not. We're horrible!' yelled the Chief Troll.

'But you're so cuddly,' insisted Luke, giving them such a big smile.

'Shut up!' roared the Chief Troll. 'We're horrible, horrible, horrible!'

Luke shook his head and repeated quietly, 'Cute!'

'Aargh!' screamed the Chief Troll. 'We are horrible!' and he flew into such a rage that he exploded on the spot. BANG!

The other trolls ran away.

Soon after this, Luke reached the top of the mountain and he walked into the castle and found the Princess Ramona, who was every bit as beautiful as everyone had said.

'Great heavens above,' cried Ramona, 'someone has actually made it to the top of the mountain and he's rather gorgeous – despite the totally untrendy clothes and strong smell of garlic.'

For the sake of decency and so on I am going to leave out the bit where they fall in love and have a smooch, but they did all that and then Luke said it was time to go back down the mountain.

'But I can't,' said Ramona. 'There's a witch down there, and a bear and trolls and all sorts of horrible creatures and brambles and I might tear my dress.'

'We can't stay up here for ever,' said Luke. 'Down there, at the bottom of the mountain, that is where the rest of the world starts and there is so much to see and to do and I am going to see it and do it and I want you to be with me.'

'I dearly want to see the rest of the world,' murmured Ramona. 'And I want to be with you more than anything else.'

But Ramona was very frightened and she would not go down the mountain. Luke eventually set off on his own. 'I shall wait for one day,' he told her. 'After that I shall set off on my own if you have not arrived. You must make up your mind Ramona. You must overcome your own fear. I cannot do that for you.'

Halfway down the mountain Luke met the trolls again. 'Cute,' he smiled and this time they hid under rocks before any more of them could explode. He met the Black Bear but the salami was finished so he gave the bear a salad sandwich instead.

'Hmmm, nice,' said the bear. 'People often forget that bears are omnivores. I love eating greens.'

Next up was the Waggletooth Witch, who simply blushed and smiled and fluttered her eyelashes. Luke got away with blowing her a kiss and after that he reached the bottom of the mountain without any further problems. He never did see the Giant Man-Eating Unicorn That Nobody Had Ever Seen, which didn't surprise Luke but did surprise all the villagers when they asked what had happened.

Meanwhile, on top of the mountain, Ramona gazed back down towards the village. And she wondered. *Did she dare?* She desperately wanted to be with Luke and to explore the world and escape from her horrible castle.

But – was her love strong enough to overcome her fears?

And – if she did overcome her fears and she set off down the mountain, how would she deal with the Waggletooth Witch and the trolls and the bear and the brambles? Would she be as wise and kind as Luke?

You see, this story does not have a fairy-tale ending, because it isn't a fairy tale. In real life there are always problems, and *you* have to solve them.

THE END

Epilogue

Why isn't this a fairy tale? Because it hasn't got any fairies in it. In fact, do you know ANY fairy tales that HAVE got fairies in them?

CELIA REES

under the skin

Chris Thompson had been looking forward to this for weeks,
everybody had. The bus had buzzed with excitement all the way
to London. Mrs Jones had lined them all up outside, barking out
orders: 'No eating, no running, no mobiles, no talking loudly.'
She'd let them file past her two at a time, holding a bag for them
to spit their chewing gum into, and then they'd had to wait in
another line, but now they were finally inside.

The first room they came into contained a video installation.
They had missed the beginning. A computer simulation showed
a city on an island in the centre of a lake. Pyramids grew inside
it, the first one small, the next bigger, then bigger and bigger,
until the whole lot fell away and other cities grew up, one on top
of another. The last was new, a modern city that spread and
spread until the lake disappeared altogether under a sprawl of
modern buildings. The effect was quite hypnotic, like watching a
silent film. The end was an eagle on a cactus, a snake in its
beak.

'The founding myth of the Aztecs is still the emblem of
Mexico City today.' Del read. 'That was crap,' he said to Chris.
'You'd think they could get better graphics than that. Don't show
sacrifices, or nothing. Just buildings.' He looked around.

'Without them headphone things, it don't mean anything, and we can't have those 'cos they're too dear. C'mon.' He pulled Chris's arm. 'Let's go see the rest of it. Maybe they've got more stuff about sacrificing and that in there.'

The sacrifices had been the object of everyone's fascination. The classroom walls were plastered with so many lurid and bloody depictions that they had practically run out of red paint. Mrs Jones had finally banned any further offerings and made people paint corncobs and cacao pods: 'To show how the Aztecs *really* lived.'

Chris and Del followed the directional arrows into a series of large rooms lit by dim, diffused light. The subdued lighting was to protect the artefacts, Chris guessed, but it gave a weird kind of reddish tinge to everything. Chris wondered if that was deliberate. A reminder of blood. The shadowiness added to the mystery and strangeness of the artefacts on display: faces carved from polished stone gleamed as if sweat sheened; sharp eyes of black obsidian glittered as if they were still watching; huge stone reliefs showed intricate patterns of glyphs, like graffiti gouged by gods into living rock. Such subtlety was lost on most of his classmates who were ignoring Mrs Jones's instructions about not running and shouting and were buzzing about everywhere getting looks from the other visitors and scowls from the attendants. They'll be out the other end in no time, Chris thought, looking at his watch. They had hours yet, but lots of people just liked to steam through then hang about in the shop.

'C'mon, man!' Del was bouncing up and down next to him as Chris stopped to read one of the wall panels. 'This bit's boring. There's a better place further up.' He bobbed about trying to see into the next room. 'There's a guy up there with all his guts hanging out!'

'You go on, then,' Chris said. 'I'll see you later.'

'OK. You sure?'

'Yeah. It's OK.' Chris preferred to be on his own, anyway. 'I'll be fine.'

Del shrugged. Chris was all right, and his best mate, but he was in 'Gifted and Talented' for Humanities and all kinds of other subjects, which probably accounted for his interest in this kind of stuff.

All they wanted was the sacrifices. To see the knife plunge in, the heart torn out, still beating, the blood pouring out of bodies, cascading down the pyramids, watch the warm sticky flow go black, hear the buzz of the flies descending, smell the coppery stink turning to cloying decay. The horror was what they came for, and when they did not see it all laid out like that, they felt cheated somehow and quested from room to room in search of it, until they came out at the other end, vaguely dissatisfied, and drifted off to the shop to buy skull-shaped rubbers and pyramid pencil sharpeners.

The horror was there. You just needed to know how to look.

A huge Chacmool stood in front of him. Even the name seemed to have a blunt brutality about it. The figure lounged with casual indifference, its midriff a hollow basin ready to receive the pulsing human heart. Even the way the Aztecs saw hearts was different. When *we* draw, or carve them, they are – well – heart-shaped: symbols of love, valentines, anniversaries. The Aztec heart was anatomically more correct: cowled with blood vessels, fat and bulbous, the top bulging with valves and trailing pipes, as though just torn from its seat in the human chest.

There was a strangeness about some of the figures, the gods, that Chris found both fascinating and repellent. They sucked him in to look at them again, but what he saw made him turn away, almost in dismay. These were the faces of the living dead, with the tangled, matted hair of a buried corpse, lips pulled back from rows of teeth, claw-like hands with long curving nails reaching out to grab and tear. The detail was exact. Don't they say that nails and hair grow in the grave? It was as if real corpses had been dug up to be used as models. You could almost smell the decay coming off the dry, dusty stone surface.

The next figure he came to was the strangest of all. It was not like anything Chris had ever seen before. It had too many hands for a start, and the features of the face were not very clear; it was like looking at a sculpture with double exposure. Chris had to lean in closely to see what he was actually looking at and still wasn't sure. He glanced down at the little notice under the figure. *Xipe Totec: our flayed lord*. A mouth inside another mouth, empty lids, gaping slits in the skin, contained other eyes. An extra pair of hands dangled from the wrists, as empty and useless as winter mitts.

Chris stared in a kind of horrified curiosity. There was another person in there. His hands, neck, lips and mouth showed a vivid living red against the rough grey stone.

Chris scanned the written description on the wall behind, then he leaned closer, as close as he could get without triggering the alarms. The eyes inside the skin mask were shiny black, the whites bloodshot from drinking pulque: an alcoholic drink fermented from cactus juice. The skin-suit had been sutured up the back and behind the head; crude stitching across the chest showed that the skin had come from a sacrificed victim. The boy inside looked frightened. The lips within the lips were drawn back from the teeth. The black eyes wide and staring, whites reddened by the drink he'd taken to give him courage.

Chris tried to imagine what it would be like to be sewn into a suit like that: like a wet suit perhaps, but then not like that at all. Warm at first, and kind of slippery. Then cold and flubbery, then, drying in the hot sun, cleaving itself to the wearer, dead skin over living, drying to the shape, taking on this greyish tinge, as it tightened and tightened...

Chris felt his chest tighten with sympathy. Suddenly he could not breathe. He stepped away, grabbing his inhaler, applying it to his mouth, hoping no one had noticed...

'Are you all right, Christopher?'

'I'm fine,' he managed to wheeze.

'Well, you don't look it.' Mrs Jones had spotted him just in time, as far as she was concerned. His asthma was obviously flaring up again, thank God he had his inhaler with him. She craned around, looking for somewhere to park him. 'Why don't you go and sit down in there until you feel better?'

Chris knew it was useless to protest. Mrs Jones had made up her mind. He was going back to the video room and that was that...

He is at the top of the Great Temple, standing at the very centre of the universe. Incense smoulders in the burners set around the altar. The white, perfumed smoke makes him feel light-headed. He breathes more of it in until he almost chokes. The thick, cloying aroma mixes with the hot metallic smell of fresh blood and the musky, decaying stench from the flayed skin he is wearing. The skin has dried and tightened around him; grey-white against the darker flesh of his body, which pulses and bulges at neck, wrists and hands, where the bandaging skin does not constrict.

There have been many sacrifices. The steps of the pyramid are slick with blood, the basins set to receive the offerings are overflowing. The gods gave themselves, so that men may live. In turn men must die, so that the gods can live again. It is a cycle that cannot be broken, for the gods give life to the earth and everything on it. Without the gods, the sun that sinks each day would never rise again. Men would never see the returning light, but would live in perpetual darkness, ruled by the terrifying beings of the night. Sacrifice is more necessary than ever now,

for these are troubled times. It is the First Year of the Reed, and
there have been many predictions of disaster, comets sighted,
and now islands float across the Eastern Sea with clouds caught
in the trees and strangers sitting in the branches.

The strangers have white skin, long hair about their ears and
thick beards. Some say that it is Quetzalcoatl, the plumed
serpent god, the lost one, come back again. For this is the year
predicted for his returning, and when the strange white men
landed, they set foot on the exact same spot from which the god
had departed. Or so it is reported. Strange rumours sweep the
city that the great king, Motecuhzoma, is held prisoner and the
strange men are coming towards the city, riding on the backs of
huge beasts. In these difficult times, great sacrifice is called for.
Greater sacrifice than the killing of prisoners taken in the Flowery
Wars. The greatest sacrifice of all. The sacrifice of a god.

The priests come to him. They serve the sun god,
Huitzilopochtli, the left-sided humming bird, and are dressed in the
gorgeous capes of their lord, made with feathers that shimmer and
shine, blue, green, silver and black in the sun god's eye. Their
leader wears a tall headdress, gleaming with gold leaf, splendid
with the red and green feathers of the scarlet macaw and quetzal
bird. In his hand he holds the *tecpatl*, the sacrificial knife.

He does not look at the approaching priest. Instead he looks
to the east, to the path that he must take. He will join others on
their journey to the sun, warriors and other sacrificed ones, for it
will be their duty now to accompany the god as he rides across

the sky. Far in the distance, he sees a tiny flash of red, then another. It is not lightning, and the sound is too small to be thunder. He is reminded of the flames that sometimes show when the sacred mountain smokes and spews fire.

They come to him now, leading him to the *téchcatl*, the sacred stone slab. He is in the sight of the god, but he shows no fear. Only the hands that are not his tremble ever so slightly as they dangle from his wrists.

He is held, back arched over the altar. The priest stands above him, the flint knife clasped in both hands. He expects the cut, the great punching blow which will open his chest so that the priest can reach in and take the still beating heart, the precious eagle cactus fruit, and offer it to the sun, then place it in the *cuauhxicalli*, the eagle vessel. He will soon be eagle man, his body spread like a star. He stares up in wonder at the blueness above him and feels as though he is already beginning his journey. He neither sees the knife rising, nor feels its descent, for he is ascending into the sky. A great eagle, the spirit companion of Huitzilopochtli, has seized him like a snake in his beak and is bearing him upwards, so high that he can see the darkness that lies at the rim of the world. The Eastern Sea is edged with a blackness that glitters like the blade of a black glass knife. Over the water come the wooded islands, more and more of them, crowding towards the shore. Over the land, a great army is approaching. Breastplates and headdresses wink like stars in the daytime; the warriors so numerous that they look like a moving cornfield, the pointed leaves flashing in the sun.

Boy and eagle rise higher, spiralling far above the land spread out beneath them until the great city itself seems to fade. The high temples and wide plazas, great palaces and spacious villas, market places, ball courts and processional ways are all gone. They are replaced by other buildings which grow and spread, outwards and ever outwards, until the vast lake disappears under them. Now it is hard to see. Even up here the air grows misty. The eagle hovers for a few moments, then opens his beak. With one beat of his great wings he turns and flies towards the mountains, leaving the snake falling, falling towards the earth...

'We're off. Wanna go to the shop?'

Chris jolted upright to see Del looking down at him. He almost didn't recognise him.

'No,' he shook his head. 'I'm good.'

'You were nearly asleep,' Dell laughed.

'Kind of,' Chris looked sheepish.

'Not surprised. That video was rubbish. Enough to send anyone off. Come on,' Del broke into a trot. 'Jones is rounding 'em all up. Don't want to miss the bus.'

'What did you think?' Mrs Jones asked as the bus started.

'It was OK,' Del considered. 'But taken as a whole, I think the Aztecs were pretty crap.'

They were sitting up at the front so Mrs Jones could keep an eye on Chris.

'Oh, why's that?' Mrs Jones asked, glad that the trip had made them think, made them want to talk about what they had just seen, even if the words used were, well, ever so slightly negative.

''Cos they couldn't even invent a wheel,' he said.

'Or steel,' Roger Brightman joined in. 'No wonder they got hammered by that Spanish geezer.'

'Yeah. Did you see the knives they had? Great clumsy flint things. Primitive!' Del said. 'How were they supposed to fight with those?'

'The knives weren't for fighting.' Chris spoke up next to him. 'They were made that way so that they could punch through the breastbone of a man, cut through the ribcage. They were good for that. As good as any surgeon's saw nowadays.'

'That right?' Del asked.

'Yeah, that's right.'

Chris turned away from him, staring out of the window. Del settled back in his seat to think about what his friend had just told him. That's why he liked Chris. That's why Chris was his mate – might act weird sometimes, but he really got under the skin of a thing. Hard to say how exactly, but he knew some seriously cool stuff.

ROS ASQUITH

the cherry pie

ILLUSTRATIONS BY ROS ASQUITH

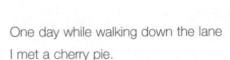

One day while walking down the lane
I met a cherry pie.
'Hello,' I said.
It shook its head
so 'Cheerio' said I.

But damply dripping from its crust
I noticed one small tear.
I took it home,
I warmed it up,
it soon was full of cheer.

'How are you now, dear Cherry Pie?'
I asked, after a while.
'Crisply crump,'
the pie replied
– and smiled a grateful smile.

It looked so cheerful sitting there
– so sweet, so very nice –
that while it hummed
a song of thanks
I quietly cut a slice.

Now harken to me cherry pies!
Walk not in lanes when you are glum.
Or if you must
then dry your crust,
else you'll be eaten
– every crumb.

RACHEL COHN

the last halloween

ILLUSTRATIONS BY ANDI GOOD

Orchard Grove wasn't called 'the suburban United Nations' just because its residents came from all over the world. Orchard Grove also had Monica, the Ambassador of Halloween. Monica had Orchard Grove's suburban sprawl of apartment buildings, condos, townhouses and basic cookie-cutter homes that looked like Monopoly houses mapped out like a four-star general's battle plan. This was her last Halloween for trick-or-treating, and Monica intended to go out with a bang.

The divorced dads in the condos on the eastern edge, near the strip mall, could be counted on for guilt candy, and good candy too – regular sized, not mini – Reese's and Snickers and M&M's. They could also be counted on for giving out piles and piles of candy, especially if the trick-or-treater at their doorstep resembled their son or daughter who was trick-or-treating across town with Mom because this year Dad got Thanksgiving with the kids but Mom got Halloween, with Christmas and New Year still under negotiation.

The single moms in the apartment buildings to the north were not always the best bet; too many of them had disturbing tendencies to hand out healthy treats like boxes of raisins and granola bars, which made Monica want to say *Why bother?* to them instead of the required *thank-you*-with-a-smile. Any wise commander of Halloween knew that only minimal time should be spent passing through the single moms' buildings.

The retired couples in the one-storey cookie-cutter homes to the west, near the community pool, were a mixed bet. They were admittedly big with the quality hard candy – Jolly Ranchers and Charm Pops and Gobstoppers – although some also gave out a weird hard candy concoction called Coffee Nip that only Mommy would eat. But even after all their years of doling out Halloween treats, some of the old-timers still hadn't figured out that moms would confiscate any home-made cookies or caramel apples and throw them away unless the moms personally knew the treat-givers. Monica thought the senior citizens should receive rule-sheet flyers in their mailboxes every year before Halloween, since they were so old they might have forgotten the basics:

Rule 1

All candy must be individually wrapped and sealed for Inspector Mom's inspection and satisfaction;

Rule 2

Any personally prepared baked goods will be promptly discarded by Inspector Mom because at some point in history some kid received a caramel apple with a razor blade in it and all kids the world over were forever being reminded about it and forbidden superior goodies like homemade chocolate cupcakes with mountains of orange icing and black, white and orange candy corns nestled on top... sigh, such a shame;

Rule 3

For treat-givers who may have forgotten to buy the individually wrapped and sealed candy that meets Inspector Mom's approval, handing out cold hard cash will do just fine instead, thank you very extremely much.

The middle centre of Orchard Grove, where Monica and her family lived in a two-storey home that also looked like a Monopoly house, just bigger and made of wood and not green plastic, was the sucker's choice for trick-or-treating, in Monica's opinion. Hers was the middle island of Orchard Grove homes, with bikes on the lawns, fake cobwebs installed in the trees, and carved pumpkins with flickering candles lining sidewalks. In this part of town, moms and dads who were dressed up like witches and hockey players greeted trick-or-treaters with not very scary *Mwaa-ha-ha* sounds. According to Monica's battle plan, her family's part of Orchard Grove was strictly a no-no for trick-or-treating purposes. First of all, too many kids equalled too much competition. Second, the moms and dads who answered the door asked too many questions about costumes and school: *And who are you supposed to be, young lady?* or *You take karate at Mister Yee's, oh you must know my little Timmy then!* Monica preferred just to take the candy and be on her way. No offence dude.

The greatest booty of all, of course, came from the DINKs, the Double-Income-No-Kids couples who lived in the townhouses at the southern tip of Orchard Grove, with the easy access to the freeway. The DINKs had mountains of chocolate bars and Gummi Bears and Monica's fave, Dem Bones, which tasted like Sweet Tarts, but were scarier-looking and yummier, and only available at Halloween time. The DINKs got the smallest ratio of trick-or-treaters to candy, owing to their location at the farthest reach of Orchard Grove, near the freeway where moms didn't want their kids trick-or-treating anyway on account of the smog or whatever. Plus, and this was the major bonus, the DINKs usually had fancy parties to go to by eight in the evening, so if you hit them up at approximately seven-thirty, at the end of a Halloween trick-or-treating tour of duty, the DINKs practically spilled their whole bowls of candy into the trick-or-treaters' bags, because they were always concerned about having too much leftover candy that would require them to spend more time at the step-aerobics class. Gotta love the DINKs!

Most of her friends had retired from trick-or-treating last year, so Monica was on her own for the adventure this year. Monica didn't think anyone *ever* could be too old for a night of receiving free candy, but it was true that now that she had graduated into a training bra, and now that she was taller even than the coach of her sixth-grade basketball team (who was pretty short for a guy, but still), well it was just a fact that adults tended to look at Monica like she was no longer a kid – mostly 'cos they had to look up at her now, not down or even face-to-face. Monica thought it just plain rude when adults answered the door and said, 'Aren't you a little old to be trick-or-treating?' Hardee-har-har. *No!* Monica didn't mind so much looking grown-up when she could sneak herself and her friends into PG-13 movies at the mall because no ticket salesperson questioned her like they still did Dave, her older brother who was fourteen and thought he was so great with his three stands of baby moustache. Even Dave couldn't get unquestioned movie access the way Monica could.

Dave had retired from Halloween trick-or-treating exactly three years ago, and every year since Monica had had to hear about his unprecedented '6.8 pounds of Hallo-bootylicious bounty o'candy,' to quote Dave the Dork. For his last Halloween, Dave and his buddies had gone out dressed like gangstas, with baggy jeans hanging off their butts and platform Air Jordans, wearing skullcaps with monster-sized headphones blaring rap music attached to their ears. The adults who answered their doors were so scared of Dave and his gang they unloaded practically all their candy right away and slammed their doors shut, fast. Those folks didn't know Dave and his buddies weren't even wearing costumes – that's how they dressed every day. And did Dave share the 6.8 pounds of the Hallo-bootylicious bounty o'candy with Monica? No.

This year: PAYBACK.

Not only did Monica intend to best Dave's 6.8 – she had moved the bathroom scales downstairs next to the front door so she could weigh the booty immediately upon re-entry back home – but she couldn't wait for the day after Halloween. Dave and his buddies would come over after school and play on the PlayStation in the den, complaining about how Mom was always forgetting to have good munchies in the house now. Monica would wait until she could hear their stomachs growling good and hard, and then she would pop into the den, sit on the sofa, and sort her candy right in front of them: chocolates in one corner, hard candy in another, gum over here, and healthy treats in a neat pile for the dog. She would count the pieces aloud. Would she offer Dave and his crew any candy to share? *Mais non!* as her French teacher said. Monica would slowly unwrap a Crunch Bar, Dave's fave, right in his face, folding the wrapper neatly, then licking the corners of the candy bar so Dave couldn't help but get a good whiff of the choco-sensation. She would then pile the candy back into her bag and loop the bag handles around her wrist before chomping down the remainder of the Crunch Bar, making sure Dave heard each *crunch*. Monica would wear her best running shoes for the inevitable moment when Dave would lose his mind and try to jump her for the candy.

Monica set out for trick-or-treating at five-thirty that night, which was kiddie trick-or-treating time, everyone knew that; advanced trick-or-treaters like Monica rarely set out before seven, but she needed as much of a jump-start as possible. This was her last Halloween, after all, not only was she old enough (and tall enough, grrr...) to go out without an adult, but Monica also got to tow along Bridget, her five-year-old sister. Dave would never have allowed Bridget to come along with him, but Monica knew Bridget was the crowning glory of Monica's last Halloween. Usually Monica was annoyed that no adult could resist Bridget, but tonight, Bridget's mop of brunette curls and big saucer honey eyes with thick black eyelashes would work in Monica's favour. With Bridget's kitten costume and the whiskers painted from her big ruby lips across her rosy cheeks, treat-givers across Orchard Grove would be begging Monica to take extra candy for that adorable little girl. Monica doubted anyone would even notice that Monica herself had gone a little Dave – that is, lazy – in the costume department, choosing to wear her basketball uniform, but at least *her* Air Jordans were genuinely part of her costume.

Aunt Lisa whisked Monica and Bridget out the door before Mom had a chance to change her mind about them going out trick-or-treating alone. Aunt Lisa was working overtime convincing

Mom to go out to a party at the divorced dads' wing of Orchard Grove. Mom hadn't gone out for a party once since Dad had moved out from their house, but this evening Aunt Lisa had stomped in with a rollergirl costume and told Mom, *It's time!* Monica knew even Dave would be happy about Mom finally going out, he was always nagging her about getting out of bed and not being so sad all the time. It was probably for the best that Mom didn't know Dave was not going to a study 'jam session' as Dave claimed, but was in fact going to a party where Monica knew there would be cigarettes and girls wearing short skirts and tube tops that were not meant as Halloween costumes. This once, Monica did not plan to rat Dave out.

Even Monica was awed by how perfectly her master Halloween plan worked out. As expected, the divorced dads handed out regular store size, not small Halloween size, bars of Snickers and Reese's Sticks and KitKats. One Dad even gave Monica and Bridget two whole KING SIZE Crunch Bars after he showed them the mantelpiece picture of his brown-haired, brown-eyed angel of a little girl – who did look a lot like Bridget. That was the only truly scary part of Halloween. What if next year *her* dad lived in the divorced dads' condos and was showing pix of Dave, Monica and Bridget to trick-or-treaters?

Still, KING SIZED Crunch Bars. Monica couldn't *wait* to unwrap those babies in front of Dave the Dork. The single mom buildings were not a complete wipe-out either. Granola bars and boxes of raisins *did* weigh more than Sweet Tarts, after all, so well worth the investment of time that could only bring Monica closer to topping the elusive 6.8.

Once they reached the senior citizen wing of Orchard Grove, Bridget complained that she was tired, she wanted to go home, eat candy and watch cartoons on TV. Monica had to give Bridget a piggyback ride all the way down to the DINK section of Orchard Grove just to keep Bridget in the game. Monica's candy bag was feeling almost as heavy as Bridget on Monica's shoulders, they couldn't give up now. And, just as planned, the DINKs came through, promptly at seven-thirty: *Oh, we were afraid we wouldn't get any trick-or-treaters over here, what a DARLING kitten costume, hey aren't you a little old for... well here, why don't you just take the whole bag of candy, we need to leave any minute, hate for all this candy to go to waste.*

SCORE!

Monica was so excited by the time they reached the end of the DINKs' houses she didn't mind carrying Bridget all the way home, like Daddy used to carry Monica at the end of Halloween. Bridget fell asleep on Monica's shoulder

– she smelled so nice, like baby shampoo and face paint and chocolate. When they arrived back home, Monica deposited Bridget on the stairs and Bridget's head smacked right away against the wall, still asleep. Monica plopped the candy bag on to the scale, breathing deeply. Oh please, please, all this work, all this planning, let it pay off. The number on the scale fluctuated for a moment before declaring... 6.7.

NOOOOOOOOO!!!!!!!!!!!!!!!!!!!!!!

But then Monica remembered the half-opened King Size Crunch Bar in her shirt pocket that she'd had to let Bridget sample in order to get Bridget to continue from the old-timer section to the DINKs' neighbourhood. Monica took the candy bar from her pocket, placed it on the bag on the scale, and the number tipped over to 6.9.

Six-nine, six-nine, we are the champions, of the world, Monica sang out, dancing a jig around the scale. Her bag of candy weighed more than Bridget when Bridget was born!

Mom came down the stairs, wearing her big old faded red bathrobe that was like a thousand years old and her ratty old pink slippers.

'Where's Aunt Lisa?' Monica asked.

'She went without me. I just didn't have the heart to go.' Mom sat down on the stairs and Bridget's head immediately flopped from against the wall to against Mom's shoulder. Mom lifted Bridget on to her lap and leaned over to the floor and without asking grabbed the half-opened Crunch Bar from the bag. No!

No! No! Monica hadn't got
the 6.9 certified, and
now Mom had eaten
the scale tipper.
Why? Why? Why?

'Oh, this is just what I
needed,' Mom said. She
dug in deeper to the bag,
pulling out a box of
Boston Baked Beans,
an obscure candy
doled out by one of
the divorced dads.
Mom opened her other
arm for Monica to come to her other side. Monica didn't have the
heart to tell Mom she had just ruined Monica's best and last
Halloween, destroyed the evidence that would destroy Dave's
Hallo-bootylicious bounty o'candy world record.

Monica figured if Mom was too bummed out to go to a party
then maybe Mom might not want to hear about how Monica had
broken a world record, because maybe Mom just wanted to eat
candy. Which any reasonable person could understand. So
Monica went upstairs with Mom and Bridget. They lay on Mom's
bed all night watching *The Wizard of Oz*, eating candy till their
stomachs hurt and trying to make origami out of all the candy
wrappers. Even Dave the Dork joined in when he came home

from his par-tay smelling like smoke and lipstick, and not even asking permission to dig into Monica's candy, and that was alright with Monica after all. She figured she still had at least one more year of trick-or-treating left in her, and she intended to go for a perfect seven-point-oh.

GILLIAN CROSS

a letter to the king

ILLUSTRATIONS BY JONATHAN LANGLEY

Dear King Alfrid,

You wanted to no how my mum makes her cakes.
So I askd her – but she was v. v. busy milking the
gote and feeding the baby.

'Cakes?' she says. 'What kind of cakes?'

How do I no what kind? 'Just cakes,' I say.

Mum rolls her eyes and size. 'Theres no "just
cakes". Theres barley cakes and oat cakes and
cakes made of pease—'

'I dont no,' I say.

But she dosent lissen. ' —and pancakes and
cakes with currents—'

'Stop it Mum!'

' —and you can cook them in the ashes or on the bakstone-'

'STOP!'

' —or on a griddle— '

'STOP IT MUM. I JUST WANT YORE BEST CAKES BECOZ ITS FOR KING ALFRID AND HES THE KING.'

'Oh *him*,' says Mum. 'I'll tell you what to rite to *him*.'

And this is what she said:

MY BEST CAKES – FOR KING ALFRID
(Dont forget to notiss the end bit!!)

Get
3 cups of wite weat flower
1/2 cup of buter
Rub the buter into the flower
Then ster in 1 cup of suggar
A litel spoonful of mixd spice
(v. small spoon)
Abowt 1 cup of currents

Bete up an egg and ster it in with enuff milk so you make a stiff doh. Then role owt the doh and cut into rownds. Grease yore griddle (or yore frying pan) and cook the rownds first on wun side and then on the other. Wen there brown on both sides tap them with your finger. If they sound hollow there dun.

WATCH THEM CAREFULLY!
DO NOT THINK ABOWT DANES OR REDEING
OR ANYTHING THAT ISENT COOKING!!
DO NOT BURN THE CAKES!!!

I no my mum is rude but her cakes are grate (like you!!!). So pleese dont chop off her hed.

Your rispecktful subject,

Berry

PS The baby says yore grate too.
PPS If you are not King Alfrid then you will need to rede *Down with the Dirty Danes!* to find owt how I learnd to rede and rite and how he burnt the cakes!

EVA IBBOTSON

the misfit

ILLUSTRATIONS BY KAREN DONNELLY

There were four children in the Herdmann family.

The eldest was a boy called Frederick. He had dark straight hair and a straight and serious nose and nobody ever shortened his name to Fred.

The next one was a girl called Millicent. She, too, had dark straight hair and a straight and serious nose and nobody ever shortened her name to Milly.

After that came Lancelot who looked like his older brother and his sister – and he was never, ever called Lance.

But when the Herdmanns had their fourth child, things began to go wrong. The baby was a boy and they called him Theodore... but Theodore's hair was not straight, it was curly and it was not dark but fair with a touch of red in it. Theodore's nose was not straight, either; it turned up at the end and there were freckles across the top of it, even in winter. And though neither of his parents or either of his brothers or his sister ever called him Theo (because they knew that shortening names was lazy and sloppy and a sin against the English language) Theodore was often called Theo just the same.

He was called Theo by his friends at school and by the dinner ladies, by the children who lived in the street and by the people who served in the shops. And sometimes, because of the colour of his hair, he was even called *Ginger*.

In other words, Theo was a misfit. He was not like his brothers or his sister and his parents worried about him; they were often angry with him and couldn't understand what had happened to their youngest child.

The trouble was that he was different in so many ways. Frederick and Millicent and Lancelot were extremely clever – so clever that they sailed through the entrance exam to the most expensive private school in the town and now wore striped blazers with towers on the pocket and the words *Strive and Achieve* embroidered across the towers in gold thread.

But when it was Theo's turn to sit the exam, he failed.

'You *failed*,' said his mother when she got the letter. She was not only distressed, she was amazed, and she handed the letter to Theo's father, who was a professor of Geology and could hardly believe his eyes.

'None of our children has ever failed an exam,' he said.

But Theo had. So instead of wearing a striped blazer with towers on the pocket, he had to go to the local school in his jeans and jersey – and though, as his parents pointed out, the standards were much, much lower at the local school, he still didn't seem to be top in anything at all.

There were things he *was* good at, very good: playing football, climbing trees, doing backward somersaults – but these were things that were not at all important in the Herdmann family. In fact they found it very hard to understand why anyone should want to kick a ball round a muddy field or scratch his knees on the bark of trees.

Where the difference between Theo and his sister and his brothers was most marked was over music. All the older children played the piano very beautifully, and they each played a second instrument as well. Frederick played the violin and Millicent played the cello and Lancelot, who was particularly gifted, had taken up both the oboe and the clarinet. The Herdmann parents were very proud of them and secretly they thought it would be exciting if their four children could play together in a quartet and go to music competitions and win prizes.

So they arranged for Theo to learn the piano, but that didn't work at all. On sunny days when the window was open and there was the sound of balls being kicked and his friends playing in the street, his head would swivel round and he couldn't even play the simplest scale because he was so desperate to be outside. After that they tried him on the flute and that was even worse. In the end they settled for the violin, because Frederick would be able to help him with his practice, and that was worst of all.

'You're not *trying*, Theodore,' his parents would cry, but that wasn't true. What Theo was doing was not *succeeding* which is not the same. Somehow they had to face the fact that they had given birth to a child who was neither clever nor musical.

There is nothing quite so difficult to cope with as being a disappointment to your family. When he was at school or playing outside with his friends, Theo seemed cheerful enough, but at home he grew quieter and quieter. Some children are meant to be quiet – they like to read and make up stories inside their heads and being alone suits them.

But it didn't suit Theo. He was a friendly and affectionate child who liked to be in a warm huddle of people and to laugh. Theo didn't mind that his parents wouldn't have a television set in the house because he had plenty of friends who would let him watch theirs; and he didn't mind that the only computer in the house was in his father's study and was not allowed to be used for playing games.

But he did mind being a disappointment to his parents and he minded being mocked by his brothers and sister for being stupid. He minded very much.

Perhaps it was because of this that he became so interested in Coleslogget Farm.

* * *

Coleslogget was set back in fields and sheltered by an ancient oak tree. It was rather a shabby, rundown house, but there were mellow red tiles on the roof and creepers covering the walls and a stream ran through the garden.

Theo had never been there. None of the Herdmanns had. It was a house he had seen only from the train, and this was because of the weekly music lessons. The older Herdmann children were so gifted that they travelled once a week to the Academy of Music in the neighbouring town for extra lessons, and Theo went along too to see if anything could be done about him and the violin.

Houses you see from trains are always interesting. Sometimes they're so close to a river that you wonder if the people who live there fish from their bedroom window; or there is a white horse in the garden, or the house is just a single tower and you imagine the people going round and round and up and up to get to bed.

But Coleslogget Farm was special.

It had been the name of the station that had first caught Theo's eye. 'Coleslogget Halt', it said and really it was hardly a station, just a place where some of the trains stopped once in a while. Pointing away from the station and across the field was a signpost that said Coleslogget Farm, but it wasn't a farm with cows and pigs and chickens. If there was anything farmed there it seemed to be children, because there were always two or three of them running about. There was a tree house in the branches of the old oak and bicycles thrown down on the grass... and a large, brown lolloping dog.

On the way out, as the train passed the suburbs of Tadcaster and the allotments and the huge seven-storey hospital where all the Herdmann children had been born, Theo did not mind too much whether the train stopped at Coleslogget Halt or not. After all, it was possible that this time he would play his piece well enough not to get into trouble.

But on the way back he did mind because it always ended badly, with Frederick sailing through his Beethoven sonata and Millicent excelling in a Bach fugue and Lancelot delighting his teachers with the way he phrased his Chopin ballade.

And then came Theo's turn, and his teacher saying what his parents and his brothers and his sister said to him all day long: 'You're not *trying*, Theodore. You must try harder.'

So on the way back he hoped and hoped that the train would stop at Coleslogget Halt so that he could look at the old house with its overgrown garden and the children who ran about and shouted and threw balls for the lolloping dog. Sometimes he looked so hard that he felt he was actually moving into the house and that he had a right to be there, a right to escape from all the disappointment and disapproval.

It was a difficult winter for Theo. He seemed to be getting more and more things wrong while his brothers and his sister became more and more brilliant and successful. Frederick was chosen for an Under Fifteen Brain of Britain Contest, Millicent won the Overall Excellence Prize for her form at school, and Lancelot composed a sonata for clarinet and piano which the teacher said was remarkable.

It was true that Theo was picked for his school football team but, as his parents said, that was hardly the same.

Although the weather was cold, the Coleslogget children still came out to the garden. There were three children who played outside most days, and a fourth one who did not come out so often... and once on a very snowy day when the train stopped a little longer than usual, Theo saw the children's mother. She had on a red scarf and a red woolly hat and she was helping them to build an enormous snowman and trying to stop the lolloping dog from getting in the way.

But in Theo's family nobody played out in the snow, and as the long dark days passed, the cries of 'You really must try harder!' or just 'Really Theodore!' seemed to come faster and faster.

Then came the morning when Theo opened his window and realised that spring had come.

It was a Saturday, which is usually a day for families to do things together. But Theo's brothers and his sister were going to a rehearsal for a concert at school and would be away all day, and his parents were going to a meeting at the university. Theo's mother had left some lunch for him in the fridge, but it looked as though he would be spending the day alone.

For a while he did not bother to get up; there wasn't really anything to get up *for*. Then he dressed and looked at himself in the mirror. His jeans had a spot of paint on them, his trainers were scuffed, his hair stood on end and it was not getting darker as he had hoped. If anything it was getting more gingery.

No wonder everyone was fed up with him. He was fed up with himself. There had never been such a misfit in a family before.

It was very quiet in the empty house and Theo felt both restless and lonely. More lonely than he could remember.

Then suddenly he stopped mooching about and went to fetch the china pig which held his savings. There wasn't much money but there was enough. He put on his jacket and went out into the street.

The first train did not stop at Coleslogget but the second one did. He got in, already wondering what he was doing, and why. Probably he was going mad, and people would say 'Really Theodore,' to him for the rest of his life.

At the Halt he got out and walked up the footpath to the house. There was a bush with white blossom in the garden. He could hear the sound of voices. The children were in the tree house.

Theo walked on... pushed open the garden gate. Why did he think he had a right to be here? The children would climb down from the tree and tell him to go away. Their mother would tell him he was trespassing.

He went on, and it was as he had expected. The children did climb down from the tree: a boy in patched jeans; a girl with tangled hair and freckles.

'Come on Danny,' they said, 'we've been waiting for you.'

Theo turned round but there was nobody behind him and the children had stopped dead, looking completely bewildered.

At that moment the door from the kitchen opened and a woman with curly red hair came out into the garden.

'Danny,' she began... and then she too stopped and stared at him as the children had done. 'Why have you changed your—'

Then she put her hand to her mouth and gave a little cry. 'I *told* them,' she said. 'I told them but nobody would listen!' The colour drained from her face and she leant back against the wall of the house for support.

A car drove up with two boys in the back. The one that got out first had ginger hair, blue eyes and freckles. He wore faded jeans and an old sweater and was a little taller than Theo, and a little older, but they were staggeringly alike.

'Danny, be careful,' said the tangle-haired girl who had gone to stand protectively beside her mother.

Then the second boy got out of the car. He had dark straight hair and a straight nose. His grey flannel trousers were neatly pressed and he held a book under his arm, but Theo recognised him at once. Another misfit. He could tell by the look in his eyes.

The children's mother had managed not to faint. As her husband came round the side of the house, his car keys still in his hand, she said again: 'I told them at the hospital, I kept on telling them, but no one would listen.'

And then she held out her arms, and Theo walked into them.

Usually when there has been a mix-up at a hospital and mothers are given the wrong babies there is a tremendous fuss. Doctors and lawyers and counsellors are called in and there are endless meetings. But with Theo and Ricky (who was now called by his full name, Richard) there was nothing like that. Both boys were welcome in both houses but they knew exactly where they belonged.

After a while they met less often, but always when the train stopped at Coleslogget Halt, Theo would run down the path and wave, and Richard, in his new uniform with towers on the pocket, would wave back. He had already reached Grade Three on the violin, and was about to take up the flute.

Neither he nor Theo had known that it was possible to be so happy.

JESSICA ADAMS

henry's guide to the stars

ILLUSTRATIONS BY OLIVER JEFFERS

Hello. My name is Jessica Adams, and I am an astrologer. My cat Henry is my familiar, which means he can turn into me, and I can turn into him – this is very useful if I need to send him into town to get me some chocolate ice cream from the supermarket. Henry often uses my computer, especially after midnight, when I've gone to bed and there's nothing for him to watch on television. This is what he wrote last night, and I think it's one of the best guides to astrology that any feline has ever written. If you think so, too, please email Henry at wowhenryamazing@aol.com and he might even write back to you. Now, please go to the window and pull back the curtains, so you have a good view of the night sky, and see if you can spot the twelve signs of the zodiac, or even (if you screw up your eyes) the amazing asteroid Lacrimosa! This is Henry's special guide to all of these things, and more, which he has asked me to pass on to you for *Kids' Night In*.

LACRIMOSA – THE BOO HOO ASTEROID

Did you know that when you cry, Lacrimosa might be responsible? This asteroid is forty-eight kilometres wide, and it orbits every 4.9 years. Whenever it affects your horoscope, you are destined to cry either great tears of happiness and joy, or great tears of sadness and gloom.

CANCER, PISCES AND SCORPIO – THE QUIETEST SIGNS OF THE ZODIAC

Some astrologers say that the three star signs least likely to talk in class are Cancer, Pisces and Scorpio, because the crab, the fish and the scorpion cannot make any kind of sound at all (well, have you ever heard a fish singing along to Eminem?). Cancerians are people born June 22 to July 23. Scorpios are born October 24 to November 22. Pisceans are born February 20 to March 20.

AQUARIAN PUNK ROCKERS

Did you know there are more Aquarian punk rockers in the animal and human worlds than any other sign? If you were born between January 21 and February 19, watch out, because the chances are, you could be in a punk-rock band by next Tuesday.

BODY BITS

Your star sign will tell you which body bits are most likely to go wrong.
Find your birthday below and look up your astrological diagnosis!

ARIES March 21-April 20
Head, face, eyes, jaw
TAURUS April 21-May 20
Neck, ears, throat, tonsils
GEMINI May 21-June 21
Arms, shoulders, lungs, hands
CANCER June 22-July 23
Tummy, armpits, chest
LEO July 24-August 23
Back, heart
VIRGO August 24-September 23
Intestines, spleen
LIBRA September 24-October 23
Kidneys, skin
SCORPIO October 24-November 22
Bladder, bottom
SAGITTARIUS November 23-December 22
Hips, thighs
CAPRICORN December 23-January 20
Knees, bones
AQUARIUS January 21-February 19
Legs, teeth
PISCES February 20-March 20
Feet, toes

Ask your friends and family for their birthdays and work out their star signs: then you can tell them their most vulnerable body bits!

BARKING AT THE MOON
People and animals go crazy on eclipses. Watch out Sunday 23rd November 2003, because there is a total solar eclipse in Sagittarius that day, just before eleven at night. If your dad starts running around and barking late at night, the eclipse could be the reason. So don't blame him, blame the moon.

Who Gets On with Whom?
Ask your best friends for their star signs to find out who gets along!

FIRE-AIR GROUP
Aries, Gemini, Leo, Libra, Sagittarius and Aquarius all hang out together.

EARTH-WATER GROUP
Taurus, Cancer, Virgo, Scorpio, Capricorn and Pisces hardly ever fight.

PLUTO – NOT A DOG, A PLANET!

Pluto is not just a Walt Disney dog with floppy ears, it is a planet, discovered in 1930. Before it had a name, astronomers used to call it Planet X. Pluto got its name from the Roman god of the underworld. It orbits the sun every 247.69 years, spending an incredible twenty years in each sign of the zodiac! Whenever Pluto goes into a new sign, the things ruled by that sign are changed for ever. Now Pluto is in Sagittarius, and airlines, airports and travel are being changed – because Sagittarius rules overseas trips and transport. By the time you grow up, Pluto will be in Capricorn, so watch out for changes to people's knees. Capricorn rules the knees.

DEAR SANTA

You can guess what your friends or relatives want for Christmas by looking up their star sign, so they don't have to write to Santa after all!

ARIES
Sports equipment, board games like Monopoly, Gameboys
TAURUS
Money, gift vouchers, plants, flowers, expensive chocolates
GEMINI
Mobile phone, books, pens, computers, paper

CANCER
Food of any kind, cookbooks, ornaments, cushions, pictures

LEO
Mirrors, make-up, perfume, aftershave, anything gold or glittery!

VIRGO
Diaries, books, computers, pens (they have a lot in common with Gemini)

LIBRA
Flowers, clothes, shoes, bags, painting kits and brushes

SCORPIO
Anything spooky, like Harry Potter, black clothes and objects!

SAGITTARIUS
Books on weird and wonderful subjects – like this one

CAPRICORN
Rocks and crystals, skeletons, sensible gifts for work or school

AQUARIUS
Anything turquoise, strange gadgets, electrical gizmos

PISCES
Fish, poetry books, essential oils, swim wear, towels, scuba gear

MALORIE BLACKMAN
drip, drip, drip

Before Nan got ill, everyone said she was a right nutbag. She certainly had what my dad called 'views' on certain subjects. She didn't like any swearing in her bedroom. She swore like a career soldier in the rest of her house, but not in her bedroom. And she didn't believe in leaving her curtains shut after nine in the morning. She said it was an insult to the sun. In cold weather she'd go out into her garden to feed the birds with her bra around her head and tied under her chin. She said her bra kept the cold off her ears better than any woolly hat. But we didn't mind any of that because, well, it was kind of funny. My nan rode a motorbike, loved to ride horses, did a parachute jump for charity, kept two pet rats in her living room – except when she knew Mum was visiting her, then the rats would be kept in the shed at the bottom of the garden. Mum hates all rodents. So, you see, Nan was pretty fearless. Except for one thing.

She couldn't stand dripping taps.

Mum and Dad warned me and my sister, Emily, to make sure we always turned off the taps properly in Nan's house. I remember once, when I was only six or seven, I left a tap dripping on purpose. Not a fast drip, just a slow and steady plink, plink. I wanted to see what Nan would do. She eventually got up from her armchair in front of the log fire and headed for the bathroom. I held my breath, but I didn't have to wait long. Nan absolutely freaked. She went berserk. She ran out of the bathroom screaming and crying and darting about frantically like a kite in a high wind.

'Go away! It's not my fault. It's not time,' Nan shrieked as she spun round and round. I watched, terrified, yet fascinated.

It took Mum and Dad ages to calm her down and when we got home from our visit, they both raged at me for a good half-hour, they made me write a sorry note to Nan and they stopped my pocket money for a month. I never tried that experiment again. It wasn't until I was much older that I even dared to broach the subject. It was one time after school when I popped in for a quick visit. Nan had had a hip-replacement operation and it was taking her longer than usual to get over it. In fact, for the first time, Nan looked her age and very tired. We usually played a game of football or dodge ball in her garden but she obviously wasn't up to it. So we played a couple of games of draughts and then a couple of card games before I plucked up the courage to ask her.

'Nan, why don't you like dripping taps?'

Nan opened her mouth to rant at me, I think. But then her mouth snapped shut. She regarded me. 'D'you really want to know?'

I nodded.

At first, I wondered if Nan had thought better of telling me, she was silent for so long. But then she said quietly, 'Conor, some people don't believe in anything they can't see, can't hear, can't think about. Some people don't believe in anything they don't *want* to think about. Well, I used to be one of those people. I didn't believe in Heaven or Hell, or demons or angels or anything like that. Shows what little I knew. I thought believing in things like that was like believing in the tooth fairy or Father Christmas.'

'But you believe in all that now?' I frowned.

'I believe in ghosts, Conor,' Nan's laugh was bitter and brief. 'And if ghosts exist, then so can all the other things we don't yet understand.'

'You don't really believe in ghosts, do you?' I asked sceptically. This had to be a wind-up.

'Conor, I *know* they exist,' said Nan. 'I know.'

'How?'

Nan stared into the fireplace, watching the orange-yellow flames dance and sway. A faraway look came into her eyes.

'Why not?' she muttered to herself. 'Why not?'

She turned towards me. 'Conor, I'm going to tell you something I've never told anyone before.'

I waited through another long pause, without speaking. I didn't want her to change her mind. Nan sighed, then she began.

'I used to go to Ashville Secondary School. My best friend was a boy called Eddie. My teacher was Mrs Tate. Mrs Tate was tall and thin with straw-blonde hair and green cat-like eyes. I used to sit at the end of the second to last row in the class, closest to the window. And that's how I spent most of my free time, watching the world stroll by past my window. Mrs Tate always used to say to me, "Amy, you should spend less time daydreaming about other worlds and more time living in this one. This isn't a dress rehearsal, you know."'

'Is that why you do all those really exciting things?' I asked.

'Partly. A small part,' Nan replied.

'What's the big part then?' I asked.

'Mrs Tate arranged a day trip for the whole class to see *Macbeth* at the local theatre as a Christmas treat. We were all going to see the play in our last week at school in that winter term,' Nan smiled sadly. 'I remember it seemed to snow every other day that December...'

'This outing will be extra special because we'll have the chance to meet the actors and actresses after the performance and ask them lots of questions,' Mrs Tate said.

It was obvious that most of my friends weren't particularly keen on going to see *Macbeth* at the theatre. I was, though. I loved Shakespeare's plays and *Macbeth* is still one of my favourites.

'The theatre is very exciting and *Macbeth* is one of Shakespeare's most action-packed plays,' Mrs Tate told us evenly. 'You'll love it – I promise. And what's more, I've got reduced-price tickets as well – less than half price. The price includes the coach trip there and back. We'll have a trip across the river into town – won't that be nice?'

And, just like that, she assumed everyone was going to go. And she was almost right. Everyone in the class signed up for the trip and all the money was paid. Except mine...

Nan took off her glasses and absent-mindedly cleaned them on her skirt before continuing...

* * *

I couldn't afford it. My family couldn't afford it, so I couldn't go. It was as simple as that. And I was the only one in my class who couldn't go. D'you have any idea what that felt like, Conor? I don't suppose you do – how could you? My clothes were always clean but never new. My shoes were polished, but always bought second-hand. My sister and I never went hungry but we were never stuffed full either. Our mum did her best, but money was too tight to mention.

I remember handing in the letter about the theatre trip to Mum.

'Mrs Tate wants all of us to go to see *Macbeth*. It's not too expensive, she managed to get a huge discount on the price of the tickets. Can I go please?' I pleaded.

Mum read the school letter, her head deliberately lowered as she read. I glanced at Alyson who was glaring at me, sparks flying from her eyes. The look said I should know better than to ask – but I've always believed, 'Don't ask, don't get!'

'I'm sorry, Amy...' Mum began, still not looking at me.

'Mum, please,' I begged. 'Everyone else is going. I don't want to be the only one who doesn't go.'

'I'm sorry, Amy,' Mum said more firmly, raising her head to look at me this time. 'I can't spare the money to let you go to this.'

'It's not that much,' I pleaded. 'And I'll get a job as soon as I can and pay you right back.'

'Amy, a penny is a lot of money if you don't have it,' sighed Mum. 'Alyson needs shoes and the electricity and gas bills have just come in. I'm afraid we really can't afford it.'

I watched Mum, trying to bank down the slow flame that was building up into a fire inside me. But it wasn't working. The fire was growing, raging inside and it had to get out somehow.

'I hate this house and I hate the way we live,' I exploded. 'I'm so sick and tired of not having any money. We never go anywhere, we never do anything – so what's the point? I might as well just go to bed and not come out ever again. I might as well just *die*.'

'Amy, don't be ridiculous,' Mum said dismissively.

'It's not ridiculous. I never go to the pictures with my friends at the weekend because I never have any money,' I yelled. 'I never go to any of the parties I'm invited to because I can't afford to buy any presents. It's not fair.'

'Where is it written that life is meant to be fair?' Mum asked angrily. 'Don't you think I'm as fed up as you are about never having any money. I'm doing my best, Amy.'

'Your best isn't up to much!' I shouted.

Mum looked at me, just looked at me – and all the hurt and pain in her face extinguished the flames inside me in less than a second. Mum turned and walked into her bedroom.

Alyson turned to me and started slow clapping. 'Well done, squirt. Well done.'

I stormed into the bedroom my sister and I shared and slammed the door. I'd known it was a waste of time from the minute I was given the letter of consent that Mum had to sign, but that still didn't stop bitter disappointment from gnawing at me.

And it was even worse when my friends found out that I wasn't coming. Mrs Tate asked me for my consent form and I had to tell her that Mum hadn't signed it and wasn't going to.

'Doesn't she want you to see this play?' asked Mrs Tate.

'No, it's not that,' I rushed to defend Mum. 'It's just... we can't afford it.'

'Oh, I see,' said Mrs Tate.

I just wanted a hole to open up under my chair and swallow me up. All my friends turned to me.

'But you should go,' said my friend Eddie. 'Everyone else is going. You belong with us.'

'Yeah, we should all go together,' Yvonne added.

Even Mrs Tate asked, 'Amy, is there any way you could come?'

'No, miss,' I replied, wishing they'd all just shut up about it. I was feeling bad enough already and they were just making it ten times worse. Eddie was right, I did belong with them but I just didn't have the money. Didn't he understand that if I could've gone, I would've?

When the day of the theatre trip came, I bunked off school. I wasn't going to go and sit in another class so everyone would know that I was too poor to even go on a day trip. My sister, Alyson, tried to tell me that being poor was nothing to be ashamed of, but that was what my head knew, not what my heart felt. So I bunked off...

I frowned at Nan. 'I still don't understand why you don't like the sound of dripping taps.'

'I'm coming to that,' Nan snapped. 'Have some patience. Now where was I? Ah yes...'

* * *

I spent the day in the library and walking around the town centre. I seem to remember I went to the park and stayed in the adventure playground until school was over and then I went home. Mum didn't know what I'd been up to that day, so that was the end of that – or so I thought.

You see, I didn't know what'd happened because I didn't listen to the news that night – that was for boring grown-ups. I went to my room to do my homework; Alyson was out and Mum was busy using the sewing machine – so the radio was off all night. I skipped breakfast and headed off for school quite early. There were only a few people hanging around when I arrived and they were obviously very upset about something, but I didn't know them to talk to, so I walked past them and headed for the library until the bell rang.

When at last I walked into my class, all my classmates were sitting in their places already. All of them – including Eddie, who was always late. That, if nothing else, should've told me that something was very wrong.

'Hi, Eddie,' I smiled, slipping in my seat next to his. 'How was *Macbeth*?'

Eddie turned to look at me and he looked so sad.

'Amy, what're you doing here?' he asked. His voice was so strange, kind of cold and far away and gurgly.

'I'm supposed to be here, Eddie. It's my classroom too – remember?'

Eddie turned to look back at Mrs Tate. I looked around. No

one was laughing or chatting or whispering. Everyone was deadly silent. The hairs on the back of my neck began to prickle. Mrs Tate turned to me.

'Amy, you don't belong in here any more,' Mrs Tate told me. 'You must leave now.'

What on earth was she talking about?

And then everyone else in the class turned to look at me like I'd suddenly sprouted another head or something. But the frightening thing was, they all turned at the same time and looked at me in the same way. I mean, *exactly* the same way. The prickling sensation at the back of my neck got worse. I looked at them and they looked at me and not one of them was smiling. And worst still, not one of them made a sound. I began to tremble inside waiting for someone to say something, anything. The sound of the door opening had me practically jumping out of my skin.

'Amy, you can't stay here,' said Mrs Corbin, the headmistress.

'That's what Mrs Tate said,' I frowned. 'Why can't I stay? I know I didn't come to school yesterday but...'

The headmistress looked shocked. 'Amy, that's not funny.'

'What's not funny.'

I looked around. Everyone in the class was still watching me, not the headmistress.

'Eddie, what...?' I began.

'That's in very poor taste, Amy. ENOUGH!' Mrs Corbin shouted at me.

'She can't see us,' Eddie told me.

253

'What?' I exclaimed. 'I don't understand...'

'Amy, we're going to close the school for the rest of the day.' Mrs Corbin walked over to me and put her arm around my shoulders. 'I know this must be hard for you but...'

'What's hard for me?'

'Losing your friends like that,' said Mrs Corbin.

I looked around the class, at all my friends, then back at the headmistress. I still didn't have a clue what she was talking about.

'Come on, Amy. I'll phone your mum and tell her to come and pick you up,' said Mrs Corbin, coming over to me.

'Miss Tate, what's going on?' I cried, truly bewildered. I turned to my best friend, 'Eddie, is this some kind of joke you're all playing?'

'Amy, our coach overturned on the way back from the theatre. We all ended up in the river,' Eddie told me. 'And we couldn't get out.'

The moment Eddie uttered the words, the clothes of each person in the class began to drip, drip, drip. Great big puddles of water on the floor. I just screamed and screamed and screamed...

There was no sound in Nan's room except the ticking of her clock on top of the telly.

'And that's why you hate the sound of dripping taps, because it reminds you of what happened?' I managed to gasp out.

'No, darling,' Nan told me wearily. 'When a tap drips in my house, my friends from school and Mrs Tate all come and stand before me. They stare at me and say nothing and their clothes just drip, drip, drip on to my carpets – except nothing ever gets wet. And I'm so tired of them watching me. I'm so tired...'

'Why do they watch you?' I asked, turning my head this way and that as if to see them standing in the same room as us. 'What do they want?'

Nan smiled. 'They want me to join them. I should've been with them and somehow I think they feel cheated. They won't rest until I'm with them. So I'll jump from planes and I'll ride motorbikes and I'll hike up mountains, but I'll never, ever do any activity that involves rivers, lakes or the sea. Not whilst they're waiting for me.'

And then, out in the kitchen, we both heard the sudden but unmistakable sound of a tap beginning to drip... I looked around the room but could see nothing. Nan looked around, her eyes wide and frantic. And then she started to scream.

I ran to the kitchen to turn off the tap, but no matter how tightly I turned it, it continued to drip. And in the living room, Nan was still screaming.

'Nan, I can't turn it off,' I shouted. 'Nan?... NAN!'

The screaming had stopped. My heart in my mouth, I ran back into the living room. Nan was still sitting in her chair, her eyes closed. It looked like she wasn't breathing. But the thing that will haunt me until I'm old and grey, was the fact that her clothes were soaking wet and drip, drip, dripping on to her favourite armchair and the carpet below.

MARGARET MAHY

the shadow thief

'Oliver,' said Mrs McMarvel to her dear, and only, son. 'I've found just the right house for us. We're shifting in next Friday.'

'Is it cheap?' asked Oliver. He knew that, given half a chance, his mother would always spend too much money. He had to watch over her.

'Very cheap,' she said, but she was looking a bit unreliable as she said it. 'And it's right on the edge of town.'

'Good,' said Oliver. 'That means you'll be able to practise your bagpipes without upsetting anyone. Anyone except me, that is!'

His mother loved to play the bagpipes, but she played them very badly. Neighbours complained and sometimes called the police, saying that Mrs McMarvel was creating a nuisance.

'It has a sunny back garden so there will be roll-around room for Morris-the-Cat,' Mrs McMarvel continued. Morris-the-Cat heard this and began to purr. 'And it doesn't leak much. Mind you, there is one teeny-tiny thing I ought to mention...'

'What?' Oliver cried, full of sudden suspicion. Morris-the-Cat stopped purring.

'Well,' said Mrs McMarvel. 'There's one house next door, over the fence. And it's a haunted house. That's why our house is so cheap.'

Oliver relaxed, and Morris-the-Cat started purring again.

'Haunted, eh?' said Oliver. 'It's lucky that we're both so brave, isn't it?'

They moved in on Friday... bulging suitcases, great flopping mattresses, and many cartons cracking at the corners but held together with strong hairy string. Oliver had a bedroom big enough to swing a cat in, which was probably why Morris-the-Cat immediately shot out into the garden. Oliver made his bed, shelved his books in his bookcase, and wound up his frog-clock, carefully placing it on the top shelf. He hung his lion-kite on the wall, set his running shoes side by side under his bed, and tied his crocodile-mask to the back of the door, arranging it so that it could look across the room and watch him reading in bed. *Everything's perfect*, thought Oliver, jubilantly. But then his mother began her bagpipe practice. She marched from room to room playing so badly that Oliver fell flat on the floor and rolled around with his fingers in his ears. The house was not quite perfect, after all.

And, to make matters worse, that very first night in his very new bedroom, Oliver woke up to find he was being haunted.

His frog-clock croaked midnight... twelve long, loud croaks. Oliver's sheets – both the one under him and the one over him – grew suddenly cold and then even colder. His teeth began to chatter so loudly that the chattering woke him up. It felt as if someone was tap-dancing deep inside his head.

He was not alone. Oliver knew that immediately. He propped himself up on his freezing elbows and peered into the night. Yes!

There, at the end of his bed, he made out a figure both black and silvery in the midnight gloom. A swirling mist of long hair rose and fell around it. And the face in the middle of that hair was like a sort of everlasting firework – exploding, but exploding *silently*, putting itself together once more, staring around at the world and then exploding all over again.

'Who are you?' Oliver asked, as well as he could between his tap-dancing teeth.

'I am a ghost,' said the ghost. 'I am sick of haunting my own house next door. There's never anyone there to terrify, so I have come to terrify you.'

'You won't t-t-t-terrify me,' chattered Oliver. 'I'm not t-t-t-terrifyable.'

But this was not quite true. As he watched the ghost-face explode silently yet again, as its wild hair rose in the air, looping and fraying out like strings of smoke, Oliver wanted to duck down between his cold sheets, shut his eyes and lie there screaming until the ghost had gone. On the other hand, he didn't want to give the ghost any satisfaction.

'I can hear your teeth chattering,' said the ghost.

'They're only t-t-t-tap-dancing,' said Oliver. 'I'm very musical. Even my teeth are musical.' The sheets were icy by now. His pillow, in its clean pillowcase, felt like a drift of snow. 'My mother is musical too. She plays the b-b-b-bagpipes.'

'OK!' said the ghost. 'I'm going to haunt you. Watch me haunting.' It drifted up into the air, looped the loop, swung on the light, then twisted around it like a shining serpent. 'Pretty good, eh?' it cried, full of admiration for itself.

'Anyone could d-d-d-do that,' said Oliver. 'I w-would, only I can't b-b-b-be b-b-b-bothered getting out of b-b-b-bed.' But this was not quite true either. (I *am* terrified, Oliver was thinking incredulously. So this is what terror feels like!)

Then the ghost put out a long, thin, silvery hand and peeled the shadow of Oliver's lion-kite from the wall. It drifted towards the closed door and somehow dissolved through the solid wood, taking the kite-shadow along with it.

Oliver's sheets immediately began to warm up, and (after a bit of tossing and turning) he managed to sleep until the morning sun chased the moon from the sky and grinned brightly in at his window.

'You're looking very thoughtful,' said his mother at breakfast time. 'Is everything all right? Did you sleep well?'

'I was just thinking about flying my lion-kite,' said Oliver. 'There's plenty of space in this garden and there's a good breeze today.'

There was a good breeze. It bustled around the corner of the house and leaped out at Oliver and his kite. But no matter how high Oliver held that kite, no matter how he tugged it and ran with it, it refused to fly. Oliver stood looking down at it, slumped and sad on the lawn. Then he looked around carefully. The trees had pillowy shadows, the hollyhocks had long leaning shadows, the fence between his house and the house next door cast a shadow, too. But the lion-kite had no shadow and without a shadow it was a dead kite.

'Who'd have thought that a shadow would make such a difference,' said Oliver, looking at his own shadow with new interest. But right then, his mother started her bagpipe practice, playing much worse than usual, and Oliver forgot his shadowless kite. He had something else to worry about.

That night, Oliver's frog-clock croaked twelve times and Oliver woke up, shaking and shivering between sheets of ice. There was the ghost, still exploding, still drifting. Oliver's teeth began their tap-dancing.

'Did you try to fly your kite?' the ghost asked him, mockingly. 'Didn't fly, did it? I'll bet you're frightened of me now.'

'I'm shivering because of the c-c-cold,' said Oliver.

'I'm stealing more shadows tonight,' said the ghost. 'You'll soon be terrified of me!' And it dissolved through the door, its face silently exploding as it looked back over its shoulder. Oliver's bed began to warm up once more and he slid back into sleep.

The sun chased the moon out of the sky. Oliver woke up, dressed, and went to put on his running shoes. But for some reason, they felt clammy on his bare feet. The laces draped themselves across his fingers like cold spaghetti. When he tried to walk, he slipped and stumbled, and, slipping and stumbling, he noticed that his shadow legs ended just below the ankles. No feet!

Oliver knew at once what this meant. The shadows of his

running shoes had been stolen away. He had slipped his feet into dead running shoes. But worse was to come.

'Stop flopping around,' said Mrs McMarvel, as he stumbled up behind her, but she wasn't really looking at Oliver. She was too worried about Morris-the-Cat. 'Morris isn't very well,' she said. 'He won't wake up properly.'

'He probably needs a break from your bagpipe practice,' said Oliver, staring across his mother's shoulder at Morris-the-Cat, who lay on the sofa as limp as a toy cat that had lost half its stuffing. Apart from his green eyes, which occasionally blinked, Morris-the-Cat was like a dead cat. And then Oliver saw that Morris-the-Cat – Morris-the-lively-leaping-about-cat – had lost his shadow.

Fear rose up in Oliver, but almost immediately fury chased it away.

'OK!' he muttered. 'Right! Two can play at that game.' He began to plan his campaign. He was terrified, of course, but he wasn't going to let mere terror bother him. Oliver had made up his mind to haunt the ghost.

Oliver plotted and planned until he heard his frog-clock croaking twelve. Midday! Lunch wasn't ready yet. Mrs McMarvel was far too busy fussing over Morris-the-Cat to cook anything, but Oliver didn't care. It is easier to haunt when you feel like a skeleton. He tiptoed upstairs, unhooked his crocodile-mask and then stole his mother's bagpipes from beside her bed. With the bagpipes tucked under his left arm and his crocodile-mask dangling from his right hand, he shot across the lawn and scrambled over the fence, making for the back door of the haunted house.

The back door was locked, but when Oliver rattled a window, the window catch came out of the rotting sill, making a horrid squelching sound as it did so, and the window swung open. Of course Oliver was utterly terrified but he was getting used to terror by now. Up he went and in he went. The window flopped shut behind him.

Though the summer sun was hot on the grass outside, the haunted house was utterly dark and damp and shadowy. Oliver hooked his crocodile-mask over his ears and began haunting.

'Oooooo!' he howled in a crocodile-voice. 'I'm here! I'm haunting you.'

Every empty room in the haunted house howled back at him. 'OOooooooo!'

It was quite a chorus.

'Ghost! Ghost! I know you're there,' yelled Oliver. 'I'm coming to *get* you.' He pulled the string that snapped the crocodile's jaws. Snapping and shouting in his most eerie voice, he prowled from room to room. Nothing! Nothing and no one!

'Come out you coward!' he cried. 'I'm *looking* for you.' He opened cupboards and smelt mildew. Hundreds of spiders scuttled ahead of him into damp cracks and crannies in the rotting floor. He climbed the stairs and they twitched uneasily under his feet; he searched right, then left, and came, finally, into the last room of all. And there, for the first time in that rotting, sunless house, he saw shadows – the shadow of a kite on the wall, the shadow of running shoes on the floor and the shadow of a cat stretched out beside them.

'OOooooo!' howled Oliver. 'I am the haunting McMarvel, and I'm haunting YOU.'

Something stirred. Something whispered.

'Go away!' said the whispering something. 'I sleep during the daytime. And anyhow it's my job to haunt *you*, and it's *your* job to be terrified. That's a law of nature.'

'So you want to sleep,' wailed Oliver. 'Then I'll play you a lullaby!'

Hooking the bagpipes under his arm, he began to play. Oliver's mother played the bagpipes badly, but Oliver was even worse.

The ghost leaped up, exploding desperately.

'Stop it! Stop it! I need sleep or I'll begin to fade.'

'This is the McMarvel bagpipe sonata,' explained Oliver. 'And now you have interrupted me, I'll have to begin again.' And he did. The whole house shook hideously to the sound of badly played bagpipes.

'Stop it! Please!' said the ghost, and now it was begging. 'Those bagpipe vibrations are tearing me to bits. Look! I'm starting to show up in the daylight, and that's fatal for ghosts.'

Indeed it was becoming easier and easier to see the ghost. Oliver could look deep into its hollow eyes. 'You're terrifying me,' it cried.

'Then bring those shadows back,' commanded Oliver. 'Promise to bring them back tonight or I'll be here bagpiping tomorrow. My kite won't fly without its shadow. My running shoes won't run. And Morris-the-Cat just lies around, all limp and languid. We need our shadows more than you do.'

And just to emphasise his words, he played the first bars of the McMarvel bagpipe sonata for the third time.

'OK!' screamed the ghost 'OK! OK! I will. I will. I only stole them to make a bit of fun for myself. It gets very boring being a ghost and haunting an empty house.'

'Boring?' said Oliver. 'I didn't know ghosts could get bored.' He looked around the haunted house. He studied its bare walls and its rotting sills. He looked down at the dusty floor.

'I spend all night wandering and wailing,' the ghost went on. 'But there's no one to hear me. I was so thrilled when you moved in next door. Someone to terrify, I thought. But then it turned out to be *you*. I'm the unluckiest ghost there ever was.'

'Hang on,' said Oliver. 'Let's talk it over. Maybe we can work something out. I mean you'll have to give Morris-the-Cat his shadow again, but I'll *lend* you the shadow of the kite for a few nights. You can fly it by moonlight. And what if you came over tonight and stole the bagpipe-shadow? Would *shadow* vibrations bother you? Because I think any ghost playing the bagpipes would be more terrifying than most ghosts. Particularly if it played them badly.'

The ghost's face exploded with sudden hope.

'I don't know,' it said. 'I just don't know, but it's worth a go.'

'And we could haunt each other,' Oliver went on. 'That might be fun. We'll give it that go you mentioned, and then we'll know.'

The next morning (after the sun had chased the moon from the sky) as Oliver made his way downstairs, something leaped out at him. It was Morris-the-Cat, playful as ever, with his shadow leaping beside him. Mrs McMarvel sat at the table, her bagpipes lying at her feet. Oliver could see at once that, even in the sunlit kitchen, they were casting no shadow at all.

'Good morning,' Mrs McMarvel said. 'It's bright and breezy. Are you going to fly your kite today?'

'Maybe tomorrow,' said Oliver, 'Are you going to play your bagpipes?'

'I was going to,' said his mother, 'but, somehow or other, I can't get a squeak out of them. They've gone all floppy, and who wants floppy bagpipes? I don't think I'll play them any more.'

Oliver tried to look sympathetic, but he couldn't help grinning with relief.

I'll say thank you to the ghost when I go over to haunt him later today, he thought.

'I'll give up the bagpipes,' his mother said, 'but a musical person has to play something. I think I'll take violin lessons. Mind you, I'll have to practise. I'll be at it morning, noon and night.'

And, thinking of his mother learning to play the violin, and having to practise morning, noon and night, Oliver was *really* terrified.

BEVERLEY NAIDOO

a sea find (christmas day 1985)

ILLUSTRATIONS BY ALISON JAY

Scarves and caps
tightly wrapped,
we pace along the beach
one blue-rimmed Christmas Day.
Eyes tracing wet patterns on the sand
touch something glistening green.
'Some people!
Don't care do they?
Throw their litter anywhere!'
A bottle deep-sea green
lies beside a clump of seaweed.
'It could be dangerous and—'
'Hey look! It's corked!
Something's inside!'
'Open it!'
'Go on!'
Through the murky glass
a piece of paper
suggests a small mystery.
We struggle with the cork

till, popping through,
a child's words
speak out
in French!
MON NOM EST KATIA
J'ai 5 ans
Écrivez-moi s'il vous plait!
Underneath
in neat letters
an address across the ocean!
Beside us
the waves break steadily, calmly.
But looking out as far as the eye can see,
remembering night-splintering storms,
we wonder and marvel
at this glassy capsule
which has bobbed safely to our shore.

The story behind this poem

This really happened! We were walking along the beach on our
first Christmas Day in Bournemouth when we stumbled on a
mucky green bottle. It was chance that one of us spotted the
paper inside. The message in French was easy to translate. *My
name is Katia. I am 5 years old. Write to me please!* Underneath
was an address of an infant school in Plouescat. I wrote it down

in my writer's notebook. At home we checked our map. Plouescat was at the far end of Brittany, the bit that juts out into the Atlantic Ocean like a dog's nose. Had the bottle travelled all that way?

Our daughter Maya, just ten, sent a postcard. I helped her write it in French. A couple of weeks later, a letter arrived in a young child's handwriting. It was from Katia and 'Les Chicolodenns de Plouescat'. It began 'Bonjour Famille Naidoo' and ended with the Breton greeting 'Kenaro'. The children sent us drawings and wanted to know about our family. Did we keep dogs, cats, calves, pigs or chickens? Maya replied and the correspondence took off. It was a great way to begin learning French. The class had a wonderfully imaginative teacher. Mlle Evelyne le Guern sent letters and books made by the children, photographs, postcards, newspaper cuttings and all sorts of memorabilia. Maya, in turn, wrote letters and illustrated little books about us.

Katia and her friends moved on and their teacher introduced us to her next class. When she retired to an even more remote part of Brittany, she continued to write and send gifts at Christmas to Maya with delicious Breton biscuits for the family. Maya carried on learning French. During her A levels she visited Mlle le Guern who, in turn, made her first trip over the Channel to visit us. She told us about her childhood during the war under Nazi occupation. We told her about South Africa under apartheid. Her family's history is deeply Breton. Ours is full of journeys across oceans and continents. Maya is grown-up now, speaks French, loves learning new languages and she and I have written our first book together – with a sea theme! Mlle le Guern and I have grey hairs. But our family friendship and sharing of stories, that began with a child's letter in a bottle, live on.

JAMES MOLONEY

the truth about possums

My dad has a standard answer if anyone asks him whether he
likes animals.

'Animals,' he starts up enthusiastically. 'Yes, I love animals.
They taste great!'

That usually brings a look of absolute horror to the face of the
poor person who asked him. But this is nothing compared to
what happened one day when Mrs Waller, next door, complained
to him about the feral cats in our neighbourhood.

'They're getting out of hand, don't you think? What are we
going to do with them all?' she complained.

'Ah,' Dad sighed in sympathy. 'So many cats, so few recipes.'
Mrs Waller said she would report him to the RSPCA.

Dad said he would buy her a sense of humour for Christmas.

They haven't talked much over the fence since then.

Mind you, that last joke has come back to haunt Dad lately. All
because of a certain possum. Let me explain.

Our house has an iron roof, you see. When it rains on summer
nights, I lie in bed listening to the heavy drops drumming on the
corrugated sheets. It's one of those sounds that becomes a
feeling. Dad loves it, too, because I've heard him talk about it.
When he does, his hair doesn't seem so grey and his deep voice

loses the edge I once (secretly) feared.

A few weeks ago, a possum started running across our roof. It was always about the same time, around four o'clock in the morning. The run only lasted a few seconds but it was enough to wake Dad. Then he would toss and turn, getting crankier and crankier until the alarm went off at six-thirty.

Night after night, the possum made its run.

'It gets on to the roof from that branch there,' he pointed out to me at the breakfast table one morning. I could see the limb of a gum tree through the window, the end of it disappearing above the gutter. That evening, when he arrived home from work, he dragged me away from the television to help him cut the branch off at the trunk.

'That will fix him,' he said with a wink.

That night, about four, a terrific thud reverberated through the house. That set our little silky terrier, Yassy, barking. Next thing, my little brother woke up crying and shouting for Mum.

'It's that damned possum,' raged Dad. 'It jumped down on to the roof from higher up.'

'Just as well elephants don't live in trees, then?' said Mum as she soothed my brother and slipped him back into bed. She has the driest sense of humour. Think Sahara desert.

Dad had a laugh at that but I think he lay there the rest of the night thinking.

In the morning, he didn't appear at breakfast. Mum sent me to look for him. He was in the front yard, still in his PJs, inspecting the umbrella tree that stands only a metre or two from the corner of the house.

When he saw me, he called me over. 'I've worked it out. See that umbrella tree?'

'You mean the one Mum wants you to cut down?'

He wasn't listening. I knew because his eyes stayed on that tree while his hand absently scratched the stubble on his chin. 'The possum jumps from the roof on to that umbrella tree. Takes a flying leap, you see. That's why it gallops across the roof making such a racket.'

'Dad, Mum's asked you to cut down that tree a hundred times.'

He still didn't hear a word. 'I'm going to cut it down,' he muttered, as though it was a completely new idea. A devilish gleam crept into his eye. If he could have made an evil chuckle, he would have.

Evil chuckle. Who am I kidding? There's nothing evil about my dad. He cries at the end of sentimental movies. I've seen him. But this war with the possum had his blood racing. He whistled to himself all day after we cut down that umbrella tree. Dad only whistles when he's happy.

That night, right on schedule, the possum landed on our roof. It was on the move immediately, its hard claws skittering noisily on the metal. It picked up speed, racing towards the same corner of the house.

What goes through a possum's mind? I wondered. It wouldn't like being exposed on a roof like this. That explains the running.

Is it hungry for the berries of the umbrella tree? It's not afraid of heights. I mean, it's a possum, for God's sake. During the day, it sleeps high in the gum trees as they sway around in the wind.

So it gallops on, unaware of the disturbance it is causing just a few metres below. Ahead, it can see the corner of the house. It knows the umbrella tree is there. No need to look. It takes a final, powerful stride just before the gutter. Out it leaps into midair – and guess what? No tree.

Dad heard it just as I did. Gallop, gallop, gallop... silence – absolute, free-falling silence – and then... thud.

I suppose possums must fall out of trees, sometimes. Bit of an occupational hazard. Maybe they sit around when they're old trying to top one another's stories about the worst fall they ever had.

Anyway, our possum went for a buster. The next moment, Dad bellows triumphantly, 'Aha, gotcha!'

Of course he woke Mum and Yassy and my little brother, who'd heard Mum's comment the night before and thought it was an elephant come to stomp on him.

Dad helped to calm him down but I could tell he was pleased with himself. Possum – 1, Dad – 1.

Wouldn't you know it. Just a few days later, the possum was back in front.

When I was little, Mum and Dad took us to an alpaca farm. Never heard the word before? Think llama. They come from South America – look a bit like small camels without the humps.

There were six or seven in one large, grassy paddock. Down in one corner was a browned-off circle only two metres across.

'What's that?' I asked the guide.

'Their toilet,' was the answer. 'If you put alpacas in a field like this, they all do their business in the one spot.'

'Ugh, gross,' I said, making a face.

'No, it's very hygienic, really,' said the guide.

Maybe possums worry about hygiene, too. Put one in a confined space and it pees in the same spot every time. It was three days before we realised the possum was crawling under the edge of our roof to sleep on the ceiling. By then, it had peed so many times in the one spot that a stain was showing through the plaster. The stain was right above my bed.

This time I felt completely justified in expressing my feelings. Ugh, gross.

Dad rang an equipment hire company but when he heard how much it cost to hire a possum trap, he slammed down the phone.

'I'll build my own,' he said.

Mum groaned.

The stain above my bed grew larger.

It took Dad all weekend to build that trap. He whistled the whole time. Of course, I had to help him which meant being the gofer. Go for this, go for that. It's not that Dad doesn't have brilliant ideas. It's just that he can't always make them work.

There is always scrap timber lying about our place and since he was trying to save money, Dad used that to build his possum trap. It looked all right, basically a rectangular box with a gate at one end that fell down when anything touched the bait dangling from a trip wire. Simple. He added a clever locking bar that fell into place once the trap was sprung.

'What are you going to use for bait?' I asked when the trap was finished.

'Don't know. What do possums eat?'

'Vegemite sandwiches,' said my little brother.

We looked at him like he'd just taken his pants off in public.

'And they like lamingtons, too,' he added, in case we were out of Vegemite. When he saw that we didn't believe him, he frowned and dug his heels in. 'It was in that book Mum read to me a hundred times. You know the one,' he insisted, glaring at me. 'You listened to it, as well.'

They were both looking at me now. 'A book?' said Dad. 'Do you know what he's talking about?'

I didn't. Not at first anyway. When did Mum ever read us stuff about possums?

My brother was well away now. 'It had everything that possums like to eat in it, so they can see.'

'So they can see,' I muttered, and then it came to me. 'You mean *Possum Magic*! But that's just a story.'

My brother looked cheated and confused. Just a story! I could tell what he was thinking behind his eyes. *You mean, it's not true?*

Oh, no, I thought. Look at him. He's going back over every book Mum has ever read to him. *Not true. Made up. It's a trick!* I doubt he'll believe anything he reads in a book ever again. In that one moment, we'd probably ruined his life.

Dad didn't seem concerned. He ignored my little brother and focused on the problem at hand. 'We don't know what possums eat. No worries. I'll ring Herbie.'

Herbie was Dad's mate. He knew everything, like a walking encyclopedia. Who needs books when you've got Herbie. That's what Dad thinks, anyway. Herbie told Dad to use native fruits and stuff.

'Herbie's an idiot,' said Mum when she overheard our conversation. 'You use half an apple sprinkled with a touch of vanilla essence. Works every time.'

'Native fruits,' Dad answered stubbornly, and we entered into one of those stand-offs that had us all tiptoeing about the house uncomfortably, like someone was about to die.

Dad climbed up through the manhole in our ceiling and set the trap – with some berries from a bush I couldn't pronounce. We could hear the possum crawling about up there at night. It didn't go near the trap. The brown patch above my bed got bigger. Dad stopped whistling.

On the third day, Dad's resistance died. 'All right,' he said ungraciously. 'Where's the vanilla essence?' and we could all breath easily again.

Just after dark, he climbed up through the manhole again and baited the trap with an apple reeking of vanilla essence. Before we'd even finished dinner, there was a muffled slap of wood against wood, in the ceiling.

'Aha! Aha!' cried Dad. He didn't even notice the smug look on Mum's face. He did a little jig around the dinner table instead. Then it was up the ladder to poke his head through the manhole. 'Yep, there he is. Get me the torch from the kitchen drawer.'

'Don't frighten the poor thing,' Mum warned.

I'd found the torch by then and handed it up to him. Big mistake. Possums like the dark. Light is their enemy. It began to thrash about in the cage. It didn't matter how hard it threw itself against the gate, Dad's locking bar stayed firm. At this rate, Mum would have to admit that Dad wasn't such a dill after all.

Then the possum's wild fury rolled the cage on to its side. Without gravity to hold the locking bar in place, the gate opened a fraction. That's all a possum needs. He was out of there.

Later, we sat around the dinner table. Dessert had been cancelled. The silence of a family death was back in the air. 'For God's sake, hire a trap,' said Mum.

Dad's look could have killed her. 'I'll work on my own trap. Make sure it can't tip over.'

The possum crawled about the ceiling unhindered while Dad hammered and screwed out in the garage. The new, improved possum trap wasn't ready until the next night. When he brought it into the house, even I groaned. It now had outriggers.

'It won't fit through the manhole,' Mum complained.

I could tell from Dad's bewildered hesitation that he hadn't thought of this. He climbed the ladder and managed to squeeze it through, though not before he had gouged out a chunk of plaster from the ceiling. 'I'll fix it,' he said quickly, when he saw what he had done.

Mum made a humphing sound deep at the back of her throat that slipped out through her nose.

The possum must have slept in that night because it didn't come for the apple first thing. It was three twenty-seven in the morning, precisely, by my bedside clock, when the gate fell into place. By the time Dad had the light on, the possum was rocking the cage again but those ridiculous outriggers did their job. Dad was up the ladder in no time and managed to free the cage from the manhole cover without further damage.

Mum was there, holding my little brother. And so was Yassy. She greeted the possum in the same way she says hello to everything. She barked loudly.

Possums and dogs don't normally get along. This pair were no exception. The possum began to hiss. Yassy went berserk. She rushed to the foot of the ladder and jumped up at the prisoner. Dad was descending cautiously because he needed both hands to hold the cage. Yassy's lunge was just enough to upset his balance.

I can see the rest now in slow motion. Dad started to fall. To save himself he took one hand from the cage. That was enough. Down it went, the corner knifing into the polished floorboards. Forget the damage to the floor. It was the cage that mattered. Dad should have invested in a few more screws or another dab of glue. Whatever.

The cage burst open.

Personally, if I was a possum, I wouldn't hang around for a chat with the family dog. This one certainly didn't. It was off. But where? The house was locked up for the night. There was no way to escape. The possum's first reaction was to climb – anything. The curtains in the lounge looked a good bet. Its dark grey body was easy to see now. Look at that tail, I thought. As long as my arm from elbow to fingertips. In other circumstances I'm sure we all would have called it cute.

Perched on the curtain rod and hissing savagely at Yassy, it didn't look cute. With the dog's demented barking driving us crazy, the possum leapt from the curtain rod. Its target was the shelf that held the framed photos of Mum and Dad's wedding and a picture of Grandma the year before she died.

Dad put up that shelf.

To be fair, it wasn't supposed to hold a possum's weight.

It didn't,

Now there was broken glass on the floor from the shattered picture frames. No one was wearing slippers. Dad snatched up Yassy and locked her in the bathroom.

'Open the back door, for God's sake,' roared Mum.

I guessed this order was directed at me. As soon as I swung it open, the possum made its dash for freedom.

After that, Dad was taken off the case. I was Man of the House now, it seemed. Mum took me with her down to the equipment hire company where we picked up a trap made of steel and wire. It was me who had to crawl up into the ceiling and set the trap with apple and vanilla.

Stupid possum. Despite its narrow escape the night before, it still came back to sleep in our ceiling. The bait was irresistible. By the following morning, there it was, the same possum crouched timidly in the corner of the cage, quietly awaiting its fate.

'What are we going to do with it?'

Dad forced himself back into the loop now. 'I'll call Herbie.'

Mum was against the idea but she couldn't stop him. As it was, Herbie's advice wasn't what Dad expected. 'That's disgusting,' said Dad.

He put down the phone and looked at Mum. 'He wanted to give me a recipe for possum stew.'

I started to remind him about his joke. You know – so many cats, so few...

One thunder-cloud glance from Dad shut my mouth. I didn't offer to buy him a sense of humour for Christmas, either.

'Drown it,' said Mum.

Dad went white as a ghost. Told you, didn't I? Hasn't got an evil bone in his body.

'No, I'll take it over to that nature walk they showed on television last week,' he said.

'You're sure it's far enough away?' Mum asked suspiciously.

'It's got to be five kilometres, at least. No possum can find its way back that far.'

Mum made that humphing noise again.

Dad and I drove to the nature walk and set the possum free. As soon as the gate opened, it shot straight out and up the first tree it came to. 'That's the last we'll see of him,' said Dad.

That was a week ago. Right now, I'm lying in my bed with my hands behind my head, remembering it all. The lights are out but I can still see the ceiling where Dad rolled fresh white paint over the brown patch.

I'm listening too, for a noise. I've heard it twice already tonight. Yep, there it is again, I'm sure of it now. There's something up there, in the ceiling.

It's a rather familiar sound.

MARY HOFFMAN

frequent flyer

ILLUSTRATIONS BY NICOLA SLATER

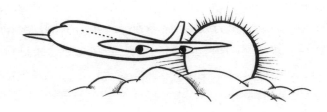

If people were homes, my dad would be a tall, thin terraced town house, with dormer windows and curly plaster decorations. My mum would be an open-plan single-storey building with a wide wooden veranda all the way round and a couple of acres of scrubby garden. And that's not just a description of the actual homes they live in – although it is that too.

It's more about personalities. My father is an uptight, edgy Polish violinist and my mother is a rather overweight, extrovert Australian radio presenter. It's amazing they ever got together at all and hardly surprising that they aren't together any more. But it's a bit of a pain because I love them both and they live thousands of miles apart. Oh – and if I were a home, I'd have to be a caravan, I spend so much time shuttling between Poland and Australia.

Not that I do it on wheels of course. I'm a frequent flyer, one of Qantas's best customers. Have been, ever since I was five, and that's nine years ago now. The first couple of times one of the parents came with me, but after that I was thrown upon the mercy of the airline as an 'unaccompanied minor'. It's really quite cool – you get made an awful fuss of and, if the flight's overbooked, you're one of the first to be upgraded to First Class. Of course, they like little kids better than awkward teenagers, but I'm pretty friendly with most of the ground staff and the attendants now.

I go to school in Australia and spend most of the holidays with my dad. He lives in a town in Poland that sounds like a sneeze and written down looks like the worst hand you were ever dealt in Scrabble. He lets out the top two floors of his house to students – violinists don't make much money unless they are beautiful oriental girls – and I have my own room on the first floor, overlooking the town square. It's fantastic, like something out of a fairy tale – all green-tiled roofs and crooked chimneys – and there are even trams in the square.

I love it. But there's not much to do there and hardly anyone my age lives in the centre. I don't really have friends in Poland because I don't go to school there. In the summer, tourists come and sit and drink beer in the cafés round the square and I sometimes manage to chum up with the odd American or English girl who's glad to find another English-speaking teenager, but they're even more birds of passage than I am and they soon move on.

In Australia it's the other way round. I have good friends at school but I never see them in the holidays because I'm always off to Sneezetown. And when I get back they've all done things together and it takes a while to lever myself back into the group. If people were tools, I'd be a crowbar.

But what can I do? If I stayed in Australia in the holidays, my mum would be out at work all day. At least playing in an orchestra most nights means my dad is at home most days, when he's not rehearsing. And if I didn't go to Poland, I'd never see him. He wouldn't come to Australia, not any more.

The first time he did, it was when his orchestra went there on tour and that's how he met my mum. He was having a miserable time at a party at her radio station and she made it her mission to cheer him up. That's a skill of hers by the way. 'He looked like a lost wet puppy, Nic,' she has often told me. 'Those big brown eyes and that furrowed brow – just like a little Saint Bernard.'

But she was the one with the brandy barrel, so to speak. She homed in on him and made him smile with her almost incomprehensible stream of chatter. And when he smiled, she was the one who was lost. Desperately romantic. Two months and two trips to Europe later and they were married and I was on the way.

My mum tried living in Poland, but the house depressed her – and it takes a lot to depress my mum. But she was pregnant, missing her job and unable to speak the language. I know, she should have learned some Polish but I think she hoped he'd chuck in the job in Poland and come back to Australia once I was born. She couldn't believe anyone would voluntarily stay in such a cold, damp, cramped little place when they could live in the warm open spaces of Oz.

The three of us tried living turn and turn about in the two countries, but it didn't make sense for their careers to go freelance and never be in one place long enough to network properly. So as soon as I started in full-time school they settled on the present pattern.

And that's why I'm sitting in the airport lounge in Melbourne, waiting to board flight QF009 to London. Again. (You can't fly direct to Warsaw.)

I still count as an 'unaccompanied minor'. My mother drove me to the airport in her 4X4 but I told her not to wait. I hate saying goodbye to either of them. The flight's been delayed but I don't mind. There's a boy about my age in the lounge, on his own too. He's frowning slightly, playing a computer game. I wonder if he knows he'll have to turn it off when we board? I've never seen him before and I would definitely remember.

If people were drinks, he'd be a hot chocolate – not that powdered stuff we get in Oz but the rich, dark thick mixture they serve in Polish cafés, like molten bitter chocolate bars, which you whisk in your cup with the frothy milk they bring in a separate jug. I realise I am salivating and pretend to bite the end of my pen. He looks up and I frown, concentrating on what I am writing. Which is this, right now.

He's the kind of boy that makes me feel all wistful because I'm not much of a looker myself. I have my dad's height and brown eyes and my mum's big feet and frizzy hair. He is sleek and well-coordinated and relaxed; if people were animals he'd be a seal or a brown Burmese cat. I'd be a duck-billed platypus, made up of bits of other animals and not sure which one to be.

Our flight is called and he gets up to board with the First Class passengers. Damn! No chance to get to know him. And his family must be loaded. I take in his leather jacket, expensive trainers and fancy haircut. Oh well. If people were cars, he'd be a brand new BMW. I'd be an old Skoda like that tin-can-on-wheels my father will meet me in at Warsaw.

And then, miracle of miracles, what's this? The Qantas boarding guy has come over and is whispering they're going to bump me up to First Class. That hasn't happened for ages, but apparently there's a hugely fat man in economy who has booked only one seat and they're afraid the person who has to sit beside him will complain. And there's another guy in First who can't make the flight. Apparently that's what was delaying us, waiting for him, but he's phoned to say he's not going to be able to fly today after all. So they're giving his seat to me!

I could ask, 'Why not give the upgrade to the fatso?' but I don't. I just give the Qantas guy my best grin and saunter casually over to the little queue which contains Mr Gorgeous. And, second miracle of the day, when I'm on the plane and turn left, I find myself sitting across the aisle from him and he flashes me a great smile. The next twenty-four hours are going to be good!

'Hello, Nicola,' says the flight attendant. It's my favourite, Angie. She's very beautiful, with long legs and long blonde hair, like the Barbie my Auntie Bridget gave me and I keep on my highest shelf, still unplayed with. I like the look much better on Angie, because she's clearly not made of plastic.

I feel I can whisper to her not to let on to the boy across the aisle that I'm not pukka First Class. She winks at me.

'Oh, André,' she says to him casually. 'This is Nicola, one of our most frequent flyers. She'll show you the ropes if you need anything.'

'Well, if I need a rope, I'll know who to ask then,' he comes back, not nastily, but with that lovely smile again. I am beginning to understand how a smile was my mum's downfall. And André – what a fabulous name for him! – is European, too. He has an English accent, not an Aussie one.

He reaches over to shake my hand, an oddly formal, very English way for one teenager to greet another. But it feels nice. His hand is warm and strong and not at all sweaty.

And then Angie comes along with dinner and it's suddenly as if we are on a date, sitting next to each other eating a meal. Only we should be sitting opposite each other, looking into each other's eyes. And not tens of thousands of feet above the earth, hurtling through the sky.

We chat like old friends and exchange our stories. This is his first trip as an 'unaccompanied'; his parents have only just separated – his father is a businessman in Australia, his mother a fashion journalist who has just landed a job in London, where she comes from. He is upset about them, I can tell, and doesn't really want to say much. He probes me about what it's like being a shuttle-bunny and I find I can answer quite matter-of-factly. Angie's right. I'm an old hand.

It's a bit disappointing to discover he'll be several countries away from me during the holidays, but it would have been too much of a coincidence if he'd been going to Poland too. At least he lives in Melbourne when he's in Oz.

He can't quite believe how often I've made this journey.

'You go every school holiday?' he asks.

'Yup,' I say proudly. 'Three round trips a year.'

'But doesn't it take, like, a day and a half in each direction?'

'Nine days a year,' I say, less proudly.

'And you've done it for nine years?'

'Eighty-one days,' I say.

'That's nearly three months of your life!'

We look at one another in dismay.

'I could have spent all that time reading, or on the beach or shopping,' I say. Actually I have spent a fair bit of it reading.

'And think of all the money it's cost,' he says. 'Tens of thousands of dollars – that could pay for you to go to university!'

I don't mention that it hasn't cost quite as much as he thinks, because my parents don't pay for First-Class tickets, like his. But he has started me thinking and I need some time to work things out. It's not until I describe it to him that I realise how unsatisfactory my life is.

The first film is *Matrix 3* but I've seen it twice already so I decide to play my tapes, because André clearly wants to watch it. That's OK because I can sneak sideways looks at him while he's absorbed in his private screen and think about the sums we've just done. I rummage through my bag for a tape and find one that Dad has sent me, marked LISTEN ON PLANE. It'll be classical, but I don't mind; it's a long flight. He's always sent me rehearsal tapes of what he'll be playing when I'm in Poland and I go to most of his concerts.

And he always records a little introduction of his own. I like to hear his voice, with his Polish accent, telling me about the music. This piece is called *Twelve Hours of Sunset*. I immediately like the sound of that.

'It is by David Bedford,' my dad's voice says in my ear, 'an English composer, still living. The words are taken from a song by Ray Harper and they are about someone flying west from London to Los Angeles. Because the plane flies in the opposite direction to the earth's rotation, the man flying sees the sun setting continuously throughout the journey. It is as if time stands still.'

'Wow!' I must have said out loud, because André looks away from Keanu Reeves and at me. I blush a bit and shake my head and he turns back to his screen. I look out of the window. It is seven p.m. – too early for sunset, but I shall watch out for it tonight. I've flown this route literally more than two dozen times and never thought about it before.

And then the music starts. Very quiet and eerie and when I first make out the words, the hairs on my neck stand up. *Half a day in the sky. I'll come and see you yesterday. Backwards in time... O how time flies.*

It lasts just over half an hour and I hear it three times before I notice that André has taken off his Qantas headphones and is staring at me. I wonder if I've been humming along, joining in with the weird unearthly music.

I take my own headphones off and realise to my horror that my cheeks are wet.

'Is everything OK?' he asks. 'What have you been listening to?'

'It's my dad's tape,' I say, and explain the idea to him.

He is impressed, I can tell. But I quickly admit that I'm not quite as brainy as it sounds.

'It's all in the music,' I say. 'My dad explained it. If I were really bright, I'd have noticed it myself after all these years.'

'Well, we can notice it tonight, can't we?' he says, opening the blind on the window his side.

Suddenly we really are friends. And we watch the sun go down together. Only it doesn't. It starts going down and then it just goes on doing it. How could I not have noticed it before? I suppose because I always put the blind down if I'm next to the window, watch the movies and try to sleep as much as possible.

Now though, I can't keep my eyes off this continuous red flare.

Time stands still. André and I are marooned in the sky. I don't ever want to come down to earth. This is the best trip.

Then Angie comes through and says, 'Prepare for landing, you two,' and I groan. André looks bemused. 'Singapore stop,' I say. 'We have an hour for refuelling.'

The spell is broken. We go for coffee together like best mates and do some window-shopping. I even look at diamond rings and have some nice fantasies about them. But we are both aware that by the time we get back in the sky, the sunset will be over and we'll never catch up with it, however hard we try. Planes just can't keep up with the sun.

Back on board we pull the blinds down and I snuggle up under the super-fluffy blanket that First Class shuttle-bunnies get. I feel sad in a way that is almost pleasurable. And suddenly, I decide that I don't want to do this any more.

'André,' I say, 'did your parents ever ask you what you wanted to do about the living on two continents thing?'

'No,' he says, frowning. 'They told me how it was going to be. My mum made it sound quite exciting.'

I can see that he doesn't think that any more and perhaps it's because of me. That makes me feel a bit mean. After all, it's his first trip. André looks really upset now. I carry on. If people were machines, I'd be a steamroller.

'Anyway, I've had enough,' I say. 'I'm going to tell them if they both want to see me, they can do the shuttling themselves. Time flies without my helping it.'

And now that I've decided that, I fall asleep straightaway and get a better night's sleep than I've ever had in the air before.

I wake up and it's morning and Angie's bringing round some coffee and croissants and I look over at André asleep, under his blanket. I feel immensely sophisticated, waking up next to such a dreamboat and eating French breakfast in the sky. He gives me a sleepy grin and opens his blind.

'What's that?' he asks, looking down.

I give a casual glance. 'Oh, that's the Himalayas,' I say. 'Good, aren't they?'

If people were books, I'd be a travel guide.

We exchange addresses, both European and Australian. I don't kid myself; he's bound to have a girlfriend. But I wouldn't mind just showing him off to the girls at my school in Melbourne. And he doesn't seem to think I'm such a platypus. In fact I've caught him giving me some admiring glances. Maybe he's impressed by my knowledge of airplanes.

Or maybe I'm not such a platypus any more. Maybe, in the course of chasing this one special sunset, I've decided what to be – not a half-European, half-Australian hybrid. Just Nicola, a girl with her feet on the ground and her only flights in future those of fancy.

A girl who lives with her mum and whose dad doesn't visit very often because he doesn't like leaving Europe. And a girl with three months of catching up to do. Maybe some of it with André. Maybe we could watch the sun set properly together in Melbourne one day.

What's the opposite of a frequent flyer? A rare bird? That'll be me. Someone that other people go out of their way to see. And it would have to be a flightless one because, after today, I'm hanging up my wings.

VIVIAN FRENCH

the mighty one's daughter

ILLUSTRATION BY MANDY STANLEY

For the first time in ages, The Mighty One's daughter is neither asleep, complaining, nor sulking in outer space. Ever since she found a tiny bare and empty world spinning round and round on the edge of her father's infinite universe she has been busy. When she asked her father (very casually, so he'd have no idea how much she really wanted it) if she could keep it to mess about with, he laughed and said it wasn't worth much, but she doesn't care. The Mighty One has always refused to let her have a dog of her own, so she'll have a pet planet instead. She calls it Earth, because that's what it's made of, and she has squeezed and pushed and tweaked it so that now it's full of dips and hollows and peaks and ridges. She has filled some of the dips and hollows with water, and is so delighted with what she has done that she calls out to The Mighty One. It's not cool, but she just can't help herself.

'Here, Dad,' she says, 'look at this! You're not the only one who can make a world, you know!'

The Mighty One strolls over to see, and is impressed. The hills and valleys in his worlds are, without exception, perfectly finished in gentle rolling curves, but there is something rough and ready about his daughter's way of doing things that is different and appealing.

'Well!' he says, and he tries his best not to sound surprised. 'That's very good. But what about this?' And he waves a hand over the dry mud. Immediately forests of trees and plains of grass spring up, changing the look of Earth from brown to green.

'Oh!' His daughter is taken aback. 'Wow! That looks really great!' And then, embarrassed by her enthusiasm, she turns her back on her father and begins dreaming up strange bright flowers and twisting creepers to trail among the trees.

The Mighty One is pleased to see his daughter so involved. Recently she has done little other than sleep. When she is awake she nags him incessantly. 'I want a dog, Dad. It gets lonely, y'know? I want something to talk to. Why won't you get me a dog?' When The Mighty One explains that a dog would be for infinity, and that he doesn't think she's ready for such responsibility, she shrugs off any attempts at further conversation and mooches moodily off into outer space. The Mighty One knows that this is to be expected at her age, but that doesn't make it any easier to deal with.

He tempts fate by sitting down beside her, and showing her how to squeeze and pinch Earth's clay into the shapes of little creatures. She is surprisingly receptive. When they are finished he snaps his fingers to bring them to life, and she is amused by their antics. She begins to model her own strange animals and fish and birds, and The Mighty One sets them jumping and

swimming and flying. The only time he frowns and says a sharp 'NO! NOT like that!' is when she begins making a being like herself, with two legs and two arms and no tail. His daughter, most surprisingly, doesn't seem to mind. She puts down her piece of clay and blows at the surface of a lake to make it ripple.

The Mighty One's daughter is so fascinated by the workings of her world that her father thinks he might as well leave her to it while he goes about his work.

'I won't be long,' he tells her.

She doesn't look up. 'OK, Dad. Hey – bring me back a dog!' She goes on blowing tidal waves across her lake.

Her father blows her a kiss, and strides off to check that his own many perfect worlds are spinning correctly on their axes. As he swings past a galaxy of tumbling stars, it occurs to him that he hasn't thought to warn her against giving her world the unpredictable gift of time. He pauses for a moment, considering. In the worlds of his making everything is always the same; there are no beginnings, no middles, no ends. The plants are always green, the flowers always bloom. The creatures he carefully crafts and then snaps into life never change. He makes family groups because he likes to see the little ones rolling and tumbling about, but none of the little ones will ever grow bigger. The adults never age, never fade, never fall apart. Sometimes their fur or feathers look a little dusty, and he blows softly to refresh them, but it isn't necessary. The Mighty One smiles to himself. They are his creatures, and they have no choice other than to behave as he has ordained. It is all perfectly balanced, all very satisfactory.

But if they lived with time...

The Mighty One stops smiling, and a chill passes over him. Time. Time passing would mean growth, and with growth would come decay. There would be birth, and there would also, for the first time, be death. The creatures would know fear, and that would make them behave in ways that could become dangerous...

The Mighty One shakes his head. What is he thinking of? His daughter is not much more than a child herself. Why, she hardly knows the meaning of time. Look how long she sleeps! All will be well, he tells himself. For certain, all will be well. But, as he steps away into infinity, he decides that he will have a closer look at that little plaything, Earth, on his return.

As soon as his shadow has left the edge of the universe, The Mighty One's daughter moves swiftly to search for her cast-aside piece of clay. Quickly she rolls and twists it; a body, a head, two legs, two arms, and no tail. She likes the look of it and makes more. Some of her creations are tall, and some small. 'Earth boys,' says The Mighty One's daughter. 'Earth girls. Earth babies.' With a wry smile she takes up the leftover scraps. 'Earth dogs,' she says as her fingers twist and roll the clay. 'At least all of you will have something to keep you company.' She carefully positions a dog beside each Earth girl and boy, and snaps her fingers with a flourish. Nothing happens. She is taken aback for a moment – then has another idea. She bends very close to her little figures, and breathes on them.

There is no significant crash of thunder, or noteworthy jag of lightning. Instead, the two-legged creatures stand up, look round, and complain because their world is too dark. The Mighty One's daughter grins. This is fun; her father's creatures never ask him for anything. She fishes about in her pockets, and finds a marble; a glittering ball of gold. She polishes it on her sleeve and tosses it into Earth's sky. As an afterthought she snaps her fingers at it, and is delighted to see it burst into burning flames. Her Earth people are pleased. They thank her, and call the golden marble 'Sun', and frolic happily in its light and warmth... but there is a problem. The sun doesn't spin the same way that Earth does; it shines for a while, disappears from view, then comes up once more on the other side of the world. The Mighty One's daughter scratches her head, but can't see how to fix it.

It isn't long before the two-legged creatures begin to complain again; now they say that when they face the sun they are too hot. The Mighty One's daughter thinks for a moment or two, then scoops up a handful of froth and foam from the sea. She fashions it into huge, soft, white pillows, and sets them floating from one edge of the Earth's horizon to the other with a wave of her hand. Her creatures are happy again. 'Clouds,' they say, but it isn't long before the tallest ones are stamping their feet and demanding that something is done about the times when the world spins round into blackness. The Mighty One's daughter frowns. She is beginning to get bored by the many requests and demands. She pulls a silver button off her jacket and flicks it up into the heavens to glow when the skies are dark. It isn't nearly as bright as the sun, and sometimes Earth's shadow floats across its silver face, but it'll have to do. The Earth-dwellers, however, are quite taken with its idiosyncrasies. 'Moon,' they tell each other. 'New moon. Full moon. Old moon.'

The Mighty One's daughter sighs in relief, and she yawns loudly as she drops down near the top of the tallest mountain. She can feel a comfortable warmth creeping through her as she closes her eyes; she doesn't notice that the sky encompassing this shining sun is clear, blue, and unclouded. She turns her head away, and curls up in a comfortable hollow.

'Hi there, sun,' she says without opening her eyes again. 'I'm just going to have a little sleep...' And sleep she does, and the sun is left to get on with his daily round of rising and setting. At night the moon takes up her own pattern of waxing and waning, and in the tiny world on the edge of the universe time ticks on.

Far, far away The Mighty One is seized with a feeling of unease. He gives the most perfunctory of glances at the last of his perfectly ordered worlds and begins to stride back to see what his daughter is up to.

The Mighty One's daughter is stirring. Her dreams have not been comfortable; they have been filled with images of burning deserts and shifting sands, and an underlying sense of guilt that she might, just might, have done something her father will not be pleased with. She flings out an arm, turns over, and wakes up.

It is hot. Very hot. The sun is shining down with a huge golden eye, and Earth is burning. The Mighty One's daughter sits up, looks round, and stares in horror. How long has she slept? Her lush, green, wooded world is dry, brown, and bare. The widest of her rivers is a sullen narrow coil of sluggish brown water oozing between its banks. There are no lakes, only wide expanses of dusty, crusted mud. The trees stand stark and leafless, and the grasslands are burnt away.

The Mighty One's daughter looks closer, and sees her animals lying listless and panting in what little shade they can find. Her Earth children are nowhere to be seen. Anxiously she peers behind hills, and into valleys; at last she sees them crouched by a tiny trickle of brackish water, where a river once shimmered its way to the sea. To her surprise, not only are there more of them than she remembers making, but also they look very different. Some are much older than even the oldest of the boys and girls that she made, and one or two look almost as old as The Mighty One himself. All of them wear rough clothes, and several are carrying sharp stones and pointed sticks; they are using them to turn over the mud. They have already dug a small dam to contain what little water there is, and now they are taking turns to sip from some kind of shell. Even the dogs are given their share; a tall woman seems to be in charge of organising everything that is going on. The Mighty One's daughter is amazed at their ingenuity.

She is also seized with a sudden pang; they are so close together, so obviously supportive of one another. Some are holding hands, and, as she watches, a girl reaches out and hugs a little boy; a little girl strokes her skinny waif of a dog; a woman cradles an old, old man in her arms.

Just then a very small Earth baby begins to wail. The plaintive sound shakes The Mighty One's daughter; she must do something - she must look after these extraordinary creations of hers. She makes a grab at the sun – and screams in agony as she burns her fingers.

The Mighty One hears her. In three long strides he is with her, and it only takes him the blink of an eye to see what is going on. 'Oh no,' he says. 'Oh no! What have you done? WHATEVER have you done?'

His daughter bursts into angry hurt tears. 'I didn't mean it to get so hot,' she wails, 'it did it while I was asleep. I made some clouds, but they haven't worked properly or something – I don't know – and now my lovely Earth is all spoilt and those poor little people are all miserable and I don't know what to do and my fingers HURT!'

The Mighty One takes a deep breath. He must not allow himself to get angry. He blows on his daughter's hand to heal her burn, but he is studying Earth over her shoulder as he does so, noting the bare landscape and dry, ravaged hills. Maybe, he decides, maybe it would be best to return it to the state it was in before his daughter found it. He snaps his fingers. The trickle of water instantly stops flowing, but to his utter and complete astonishment the people of Earth are not in the least affected. They go on digging and speaking and comforting each other but, as they notice the water vanishing into nothingness, an anguished murmuring swells and swells into a loud cry of mutual agony.

The Mighty One's daughter turns on her father, her eyes flashing. 'What are you DOING?' she yells. 'They need HELP – not you making things WORSE!'

The Mighty One is, for the first time in infinity, bewildered. 'What did you do?' he asks his daughter. 'How did you make them live?'

She stares at him. 'I breathed on them,' she says shortly. 'Snapping my fingers didn't work.'

'Ah,' The Mighty One says slowly. 'I see. So they have your breath in them... so they too will have a touch of the infinite. No wonder I cannot destroy them.'

'DESTROY them?' His daughter is incandescent with fury. 'DAD! Just HELP them – or show me what to do and I'LL do it.'

The Mighty One looks at her. He has never seen her so passionate, and an idea swims slowly into his mind. 'Yes,' he thinks, 'maybe there could be some good in all of this,' and he snaps his fingers once more. The water springs out of the ground with redoubled force, and this time the sounds echoing up from Earth are of cheering and hope. The Mighty One's daughter smacks him on the back. 'Thanks, Dad,' she says. 'Thanks. Oh – so what are you going to do about the sun?'

The Mighty One smiles, and tweaks a plug of wax out of his left ear. He holds it towards the sun for a moment or two to soften it, and rolls it between his fingers. He squashes it, and shapes it, and tosses it into the blue arc of Earth's sky.

'Woof!' yaps the little wax dog as he lands on the edge of the horizon. 'Woof Woof!' and he hurries and flurries the soft, white heaps of clouds until they roll away from the horizon's rim and begin to float out over the earth. 'Woof!' yelps the dog, 'woof woof WOOF!' And the clouds gather and thicken, and huge healing drops of rain begin to beat down upon the parched and thirsty Earth below.

'Way to go, Dad!' shouts The Mighty One's daughter. 'Way to go!' And she grabs him in a bear hug of wild enthusiasm.

The Mighty One pushes her away, but gently. 'Listen,' he says, 'it's not finished yet. That little dog is made of wax. You must look after him carefully. It will be up to you to make sure the sun is never ever allowed to grow so powerful again; there must be clouds floating somewhere above the earth at all times to bring rain, and growth, and happiness to your Earth people as they go about their living day by day...'

The Mighty One's daughter is beaming with happiness. 'I'll look after him,' she promises. 'And I'll look after Earth... but when we've sorted out the clouds each day, can I take him for walks in the universe? Please, Dad – please?'

Her father nods.

'Hurrah!' The Mighty One's daughter cartwheels across

space, and whistles to her little wax dog. He looks up, bounds to her side, and the two of them run and jump up among the stars.

The Mighty One sighs. He can foresee problems ahead, and he nods at Earth's children as he moves slowly away. 'I wish you luck,' he says. 'Here's hoping that the floods and droughts don't last for too long when they come, as come they will... But she loves her little dog and, I think...' he looks down on the tiny planet spinning on the edge of the universe '...she loves you too.'

Tony Hart

ABOUT THE AUTHORS

Jessica Adams was born in London but now divides her time between England and Australia. She has been a journalist, interviewing rock stars, then astrology and writing took over. Her latest books are *Cool for Cats* and *Astrobloke*. Jessica is a patron of War Child UK and a trustee of War Child Australia.

Philip Ardagh was born in Kent and now lives in East Sussex. He started work as a writer with an advertising agency and now writes for children full-time – both fiction and non-fiction. *Get a Life* are fun fact books whilst his novels such as the Eddie Dickens trilogy: *Awful End, Dreadful Acts* and *Terrible Times*, are grippingly gruesome!

Ros Asquith is an author and cartoonist. Her comic strip *Doris* was a regular feature in the *Guardian* for many years and she wrote and illustrated the best-selling *Teenage Worrier* series. Her most recent children's fiction series is *Trixie Tempest, Tweenage Tearaway*. Ros lives in North London.

Malorie Blackman is a prize-winning author of children's books. Of her many novels, *Hacker* won the WH Smith's Mind Boggling Books Award and *Noughts and Crosses* won the 2002 Children's Book Award. *Whizziwig*, for younger readers, became a popular BBC Television series. Malorie and her family live in Kent.

Georgia Byng was an actress before becoming an author of children's books. She has written three picture books, and her first novel *Molly Moon's Incredible Book of Hypnotism* was published to great acclaim in 2002 and is currently being made into a film. Georgia lives in North London.

Rachel Cohn is the author of the acclaimed teenage novel *Gingerbread,* featuring the character Cyd Charisse, a name inspired by the author's love of old movies! Rachel grew up in Maryland, USA, and now lives in Manhattan. Rachel's latest novel for children is *The Steps*.

Eoin Colfer is the author of bestsellers *Artemis Fowl* and *Artemis Fowl: The Arctic Incident*. He has also written several books for younger children. His latest book for older children is *The Wish List*. A former schoolteacher, Eoin lives in Wexford, Ireland.

Gillian Cross is the author of *The Demon Headmaster* books, successfully serialised by the BBC, as well as several award-winning novels such as *Wolf* and *The Great Elephant Chase*. Her latest books are *Calling a Dead Man* and *Facing the Demon Headmaster*. Gillian was born in London and lives in Warwickshire.

Marianne Curley was born in Windsor, Australia and now lives in Coffs Harbour, New South Wales, surrounded by beaches and rainforests. She has been a secretary and a teacher but now writes for young adults full-time, inspired by her three teenage children. Her books include *The Named* and *Old Magic*.

Annie Dalton is the author of the hugely popular *Angels Unlimited* series. Her other books include *The Real Tilly Beany* and *Night Maze*, both shortlisted for the Carnegie Medal and *The After-dark Princess*, which won the Nottinghamshire Book Award. Annie was born in Dorset and now lives in Suffolk.

Vivian French lives in Bristol and Edinburgh but has travelled from Orkney to Oklahoma talking about children's books. Vivian has written numerous children's books including *Caterpillar Caterpillar*, *Morris the Mouse Hunter* and *Guinea Pigs go to Sea* for younger children, and *Kick Back* and *Aesop's Funky Fables* for older children.

Morris Gleitzman is one of Australia's most successful authors. He was born in England but emigrated to Australia in 1969. He has been a television scriptwriter and his first two books were developed from these scripts - *The Other Facts of Life* and *Second Childhood*. His other books include *Two Weeks with the Queen*, *Bumface*, *Worry Warts*, *Toad Rage* and *Boy Overboard*.

Mary Hoffman has written more than seventy books for children. She is the author of the award-winning picture books *Amazing Grace* and *Grace + Family,* and her novels include *Song of the Earth*, *An Angel Just Like Me, Three Wise Women* and her latest *Stravaganza: City of Masks.* Mary was born in Hampshire and now lives in Oxfordshire

Eva Ibbotson was born in Vienna before World War II but moved to Britain when Hitler rose to power. She has written many magical novels for children including *Which Witch? The Secret of Platform 13*, *Dial a Ghost* and the award-winning *Journey to the River Sea.* Eva lives in Newcastle and writes for both children and adults.

Brian Jacques was born and brought up in Liverpool, became a merchant seaman at the age of fifteen and travelled the world. His *Redwall* books have sold over two million copies worldwide and have been translated into several different languages. His latest book is *The Angel's Command*, a sequel to *Castaways of the Flying Dutchman*.

Dick King-Smith was born and raised in Gloucestershire and after twenty years as a farmer, turned to teaching and then to writing children's books. Among his many books about animals, *The Sheep-Pig* was made into the film *Babe*. His other books include *The Hodgeheg*, *Titus Rules! Chewing the Cud* and *The Roundhill.*

Margaret Mahy is from New Zealand and she became the first writer outside the UK to win the Carnegie Medal, for *The Haunting*, winning the same award two years later for *The Changeover*. Her other novels include *Memory, 24 Hours, Riddle of the Frozen Phantom* and her most recent, *Alchemy*.

Geraldine McCaughrean writes fiction for adults, early readers and every age in between. Her novel *A Little Lower than the Angels* won the Whitbread Children's Novel Award and *A Pack of Lies* won the Carnegie Medal and the Guardian Children's Fiction Award. She has twice won the Blue Peter Book Award; for her retelling of *The Pilgrim's Progress* and *The Kite Rider*. Geraldine lives in Berkshire.

Roger McGough was born in Liverpool, went to university in Hull and lives in Twickenham, Middlesex. He was one of three poets performing as The Scaffold and since the 1970s has been active as a poet and a radio and television presenter. His numerous poetry books for children include *Sky in the Pie, An Imaginary Menagerie, Bad Bad Cats, Pillow Talk* and his picture books *Moonthief* and *What on Earth Can it Be?*

James Moloney is from Australia and lives in Brisbane. He was a teacher for many years before concentrating full-time on writing. James's first published novel was *Crossfire* and his other books include *Gracey, Buzzard Breath and Brains* and *Swashbuckler. The Book of Lies* will be published in the UK in 2004.

Michael Morpurgo is the author of over ninety books for children including *The Butterfly Lion*, winner of the Smarties Prize, the Writers' Guild Award and currently being made into a film. Michael's other titles include *The Dancing Bear, Billy the Kid, Toro! Toro! Cool! and Mister Skip*. His latest novel is *Private Peaceful*. Michael Morpurgo is the Children's Laureate for 2003-2005.

Beverley Naidoo was born and brought up in Johannesburg, South Africa. She came to England, in exile, and wrote her first book *Journey to Jo'burg* which was banned in South Africa but became an acclaimed novel in other countries around the world. Beverley's other books include *No Turning Back, Out of Bounds*, and *The Other Side of Truth* which won the Carnegie Medal in 2002.

Garth Nix was born and brought up in Australia. After taking his degree in professional writing from the University of Canberra, he worked in a bookshop and then moved to Sydney. After a period travelling in Eastern Europe, the Middle East and Asia in 1993 he worked in marketing and then as a literary agent. His first novel for young adults was *Sabriel,* the first title in a trilogy to be followed by *Lirael* and *Abhorsen*.

Brian Patten lives in London but spends much of his time writing in Devon. His collections of poetry for children include *Gargling with Jelly*, *Juggling with Gerbils* and *Thawing Frozen Frogs* and for adults *Love Poems*, *Armada*, *Storm Damage* and *Grinning Jack*. His latest book *The Story Giant*, was published at the end of 2002 to great acclaim.

Celia Rees was born and brought up in Solihull, Warwickshire and now lives in Leamington Spa. She taught English and History for many years and started writing in response to her pupils' desire for exciting stories! Her books include *Truth or Dare*, *Soul Taker*, *The Cunning Man*, *The Bailey Game* and the highly-acclaimed *Witch Child* and its sequel *Sorceress*.

Darren Shan is the pseudonym of Darren O'Shaughnessy. Darren was born in London, moved to Ireland when he was a young boy, then returned to London to university. He is best known for his Saga of Darren Shan series: *Cirque du Freak*, *The Vampire's Assistant*, *Tunnels of Blood*, *Vampire Mountain*, *Trials of Death*, *The Vampire Prince*, *Hunters of the Dusk*, *Allies of the Night*, *Killers of the Dawn* and *The Lake of Souls*.

Jeremy Strong has been a teacher and a headteacher. His books include those about *The Karate Princess* and three Viking stories which were made into a popular television series. Jeremy won the Children's Book Award for *The Hundred-Mile-an-Hour Dog*. His most recent books are *Mad Iris*, *Pirate School – Just a Bit of Wind* and *Krazy Kow Saves the World – Well, Almost*. Jeremy lives in Kent.

Jacqueline Wilson was a journalist for several years before becoming a full-time writer. She has written more than forty books including *The Story of Tracy Beaker* which won two major awards and became a popular television series. *The Suitcase Kid* won the Children's Book Award and *Double Act* won the Smarties Prize and the Children's Book Award. Other books include *The Illustrated Mum*, *Girls in Tears* and *Lola Rose*. In 2002 Jacqueline was awarded the OBE for services to literacy in schools.

Deborah Wright's most recent novel, *The Rebel Fairy,* is a contemporary version of Shakespeare's *A Midsummer Night's Dream* which became a 'crossover' bestseller among teenagers and adults. Deborah lives in Surrey and is currently completing her first book for children.

ABOUT THE ILLUSTRATORS

Russell Ayto lives near Penzance, Cornwall, with his wife, Alyx, three children: Greta, Emilio and Loveday, and two guinea pigs!

Karen Donnelly comes from Brighton and lives there with her husband and two little boys. She's been an illustrator since 1990 and has worked in most areas of children's and teen publishing, occasionally having a go at advertising, but always running back to publishing where everyone is so much more civilised. She has illustrated the children's novels of Magdalen Nabb and Jean Ure for HarperCollins.

Michael Foreman is one of the world's leading illustrators. He has written and illustrated many children's books and won several major awards, including the Kate Greenaway Medal twice (most recently for *War Boy*), the Kurt Maschler Award, the Smarties Grand Prix, the Children's Book Award, the Bologna Graphics Prize and, on two occasions, the Francis Williams Prize.

Andi Good splits her time between England and California. She likes her husband, her cat, and waking up early on sunny Saturday mornings. Actually, she loves those things. But she also likes to draw and paint and write stories, which is the reason her stuff is in this book.

Griff – AKA Andrew Griffin. Lives in West London with his wife and no children. Has worked in publishing, web design, directed commercials at Studio AKA and has written & illustrated a number of children's titles. Currently developing a range of toys. Bald at time of going to press.

Tony Hart has been a well-known television presenter and artist for more than fifty years with programmes such as *Vision On*, *Take Hart*, *Hartbeat* and *Smart Hart*. In 1998 he won a BAFTA Life-time Achievement Award in acknowledgement of his contribution to quality children's television.

Paul Hess, who lives in Gateshead, Tyne and Wear, was born in Sydney, Australia. He has had quite a journey to get from there to here and somewhere along the way he has managed to pick up a lady, three children and a career in illustrating.

Rian Hughes studied at the LCP in London before working for an advertising agency, *i-D* magazine and a series of record sleeve design companies. Under the name *Device* he now provides design and illustration for advertising campaigns, record sleeves, book jackets, graphic novels and television. A retrospective book collection, *Art, Commercial* was published in 2002.

Robin Jarvis is a multi-talented author and artist who began his career as a model maker. His books include *The Deptford Mice* trilogy, *Tales from the Wyrd Museum* trilogy and his latest *Deathscent*, the first in the *Intrigues of the Reflected Realm* trilogy.

Alison Jay was born in Hertfordshire, grew up in Derbyshire, and studied in London where she now lives. After graduating she worked for a year in animation studios but found the process a little too slow. She now works mainly illustrating children's books and would love one day to write and illustrate her own book.

Oliver Jeffers is a young contemporary illustrator, painter and writer who is careering recklessly toward creative thinking with the distinct ability of being able to put words and pictures together. Born in Western Australia and bred in Northern Ireland, Oliver is a graduate of the University of Ulster, and has exhibited paintings in London, New York, Sydney and Glengormley.

Jonathan Langley. Born on a Friday in Lancaster. Grew to 6ft and moved on to Liverpool, then London, then Cambridgeshire. Now lives in Cumbria with Karen, three kids and Lupin the cat. Worked with paper, pencils, pens, paint and crayons since 1974. Loves walking, jazz, films and drinking.

Clare Mackie was born on a farm in Kincardineshire surrounded by hills, chickens, pigs, cows and horses. Her passions in life include insects and handbags and is extremely proud of being a patron of *Full of Life* – a parent led charity for families with children who have disabilities based in Kensington and Chelsea.

Chris Mould has been a freelance illustrator since graduating from Leeds Polytechnic in 1991. He lives with his wife and two daughters in Bradford, West Yorkshire. His work can be seen in children's books, magazines, newspapers and many other forms of printed matter. More recently, his work has been used in television and in feature film development work.

Nathan Reed has been illustrating children's books since graduating from Falmouth College of Arts in 2000. He lives in Clapham, a hop, skip and a jump from the common, where he can often be found playing football, throwing frisbees,and dog spotting! He has illustrated Maeve Friel's *Witch in Training* series, the poetry compilations compiled by John Foster and is currently working on the forthcoming picture book, *What Friends do Best*.

Chris Riddell studied at the Epsom School of Art and Design and then at Brighton Polytechnic where he was a student of Raymond Briggs. He has illustrated many children's books, including the prize-winning *Something Else* by Kathryn Cave, which won the UNESCO prize in 1997. His *Pirate Diary* won the prestigious Greenaway Medal in 2002. He is co-creator of *The Edge Chronicles*, with the author Paul Stewart. Chris also works as the political cartoonist for *The Economist*, *The Independent*, *The Independent on Sunday* and *The Observer*.

Tony Ross. Born London 1938. School was a mystery to me so I went into advertising. That was baffling also, so I taught it at Manchester Polytechnic. Freelance graphic designer, cartoonist, film-maker, then did my first children's book in 1973. Since then, another 700 or so. It's all such a puzzle.

Nick Sharratt graduated from St Martin's School of Art in 1984. Began as a magazine and packaging illustrator but now work solely on children's books. As well as providing the illustrations for Jacqueline Wilson's best-selling titles I also illustrate and write picture books. Won the 2001 Children's Book Award for *Eat Your Peas* written by Kes Gray. When not working I like eating delicious food and sleeping.

Nicola Slater is twenty-six and lives in the North of England with her imaginary friends. She draws pictures for books and magazines, and can often be found hiding in bus stops.

Mandy Stanley studied art at Great Yarmouth College of Art and Design before going on to do a degree in Fashion Design. Worked as a children'swear designer in industry before setting up my own company. Have designed a range of products for children. Now concentrate on writing and illustrating chidren's books.

Tim Stevens. When I was a boy I told everyone (according to my mother) that I was going to be a 'drawer', that is to say someone who draws pictures for a living, not somewhere you might put your socks or underpants. Later on I learned it was called being an Illustrator.

SO, WHAT IS WAR CHILD?

Charity No. 1071659

War Child was set up in 1993 when the terrible war in the former Yugoslavia was having a huge effect on all of the children who lived there. We have since expanded our work to conflict zones worldwide. Working on its own or in co-operation with other organisations, War Child offers practical help to children who are faced by some of the most dangerous conditions in the world. We help children, because they are the next generation and we must give them a chance to live in peace and fulfil their dreams.

This year is War Child's tenth anniversary. Since War Child began we have helped 5 million people in war-stricken areas such as Rwanda, Southern Sudan and Kosovo. Last year, War Child's field bakery opened in Afghanistan. For 8 months the bakery produced 27,000 loaves of fresh bread a day, enough to feed an entire camp of people who had been forced to leave their home because of war. Recently we have begun to work in the Democratic Republic of Congo where nearly 3 million people have died since 1998 because of war. War Child will assist the children of this country by helping them to receive an education, and as a result we aim to give them the chance of a brighter future. We are also working in Iraq; currently supporting a hospital for children and an orphanage in Nasiriyah. We plan to run emergency feeding programmes and provide children with education and music therapy, to help them re-build their lives.

If you would like to find out more about War Child then please visit our website at **www.warchild.org.uk.** You can also send donations or write to the address below:

War Child
5-7 Anglers Lane
London NW5 3DG

JEANETTE'S RADIO: HOW WAR CHILD CHANGES LIVES

Jeanette lives in Rwanda and was orphaned when she was six years old. There was a terrible war in her country and her family were all killed when soldiers stormed into their house. Jeanette and her brother were lucky and managed to run away, but by escaping had to face a life surviving on their own. Jeanette now, aged only twelve, is the lead female in her household and has to look after seven orphans. She cannot go to school because she has to tend the fields to feed the other children. Many of these child-headed households are isolated and the children feel very lonely and sad because the war has devastated their lives, and robbed them of their families.

War Child gave Jeanette a wind-up radio. In Rwanda there is very little electricity, so the radio is perfect as it gets its power from the sun and the wind-up mechanism. On the radio she and her family can listen to the news, music, education and health programmes, and even a soap opera. The radio is a vital link to the outside world.

War Child provided the essential, practical help and Jeanette provided the determination to succeed, and as a result the lives of her and her household have improved enormously. She has even managed to send one of the children to school. This is just one example of the type of project that *Kids' Night In* may fund. So perhaps you can help raise more money for children like Jeanette?

Jeanette and her wind-up radio

WAR CHILD NEEDS YOUR HELP

Without the support of people like you, War Child would not be able to continue its vital work with children living in conflict zones all over the world. By buying this book you have already helped, but by fundraising for War Child you can continue to help make a big difference to other children's lives. Have a look at some of our fundraising ideas below, or why not let your imagination run wild and dream up some of your own events to help us raise money. And, remember, FUNdraising is meant to be FUN!

Non-Uniform Day at school or sponsor a teacher/ youth club leader to dress up for a day.

Give up a Birthday/Christmas present and donate the money that would have been spent on the gift to War Child. You'll feel great knowing you have helped someone else.

Sponsored events. e.g. sponsored silence, walk, run, dog-walking, treasure hunt, performing a different sport every minute for as long as possible, the list is endless...

FUN-draising

Raffles and quizzes are an easy way to collect money and are great fun too.

Organise your own party or disco. Charge people to come or to enter games that you play. You could even have a theme and make it fancy dress.

Coin Mosaics. Draw a picture e.g. a map of the world or your favourite animal, and then fill in the picture with coins. You can also do the same with a Coin Mile by drawing a line one mile long (in a spiral) and placing coins all the way along the line.

Double/Triple your money. Ask someone you know to donate a small amount of money. This money can then be spent on materials in order to double your money e.g. a sponge, bucket and car wash cleaner to wash cars for a charge, buying the ingredients to make cakes and then selling them...

DERMOT O'LEARY
AFTERWORD

I think *Kids' Night In* is a really cool book. The stories, poems and illustrations are brilliant, and, best of all, £1 from each copy bought goes to help other kids in those parts of the world that are devastated by war. Don't forget to check out the *Kids' Night In* website at **www.kidsnightin.com** for loads more wicked things to do. I've been there, and just like the book, it's fab!

Thanks a lot for buying *Kids' Night In*.

If you've enjoyed this book why not check out the official *Kids' Night In* website at **www.kidsnightin.com** where you can find out more about the authors and illustrators; download bookplates and enter competitions; and find out how to have fun on your kids' night in. There's also the top 100 boredom busters plus loads more fun things to do. So when you and your friends decide to have a kids' night in, it will never be dull!

WAR child

Charity No. 1071659